FOR ORGANS, PIANOS & ELECTRONIC KEYBOARDS

E-Z PLAY TODAY
24

SONGS WITH 3 CHORDS

ISBN 978-1-5400-0571-7

HAL•LEONARD®
7777 W. BLUEMOUND RD. P.O. BOX 13819 MILWAUKEE, WI 53213

E-Z Play ® TODAY Music Notation © 1975 HAL LEONARD LLC
E-Z PLAY and EASY ELECTRONIC KEYBOARD MUSIC are registered trademarks of HAL LEONARD LLC.

Visit Hal Leonard Online at
www.halleonard.com

Registration Guide

• Match the Registration number on the song to the corresponding numbered category below. Select and activate an instrumental sound available on your instrument.

• Choose an automatic rhythm appropriate to the mood and style of the song. (Consult your Owner's Guide for proper operation of automatic rhythm features.)

• Adjust the tempo and volume controls to comfortable settings.

Registration

1	Mellow	Flutes, Clarinet, Oboe, Flugel Horn, Trombone, French Horn, Organ Flutes
2	Ensemble	Brass Section, Sax Section, Wind Ensemble, Full Organ, Theater Organ
3	Strings	Violin, Viola, Cello, Fiddle, String Ensemble, Pizzicato, Organ Strings
4	Guitars	Acoustic/Electric Guitars, Banjo, Mandolin, Dulcimer, Ukulele, Hawaiian Guitar
5	Mallets	Vibraphone, Marimba, Xylophone, Steel Drums, Bells, Celesta, Chimes
6	Liturgical	Pipe Organ, Hand Bells, Vocal Ensemble, Choir, Organ Flutes
7	Bright	Saxophones, Trumpet, Mute Trumpet, Synth Leads, Jazz/Gospel Organs
8	Piano	Piano, Electric Piano, Honky Tonk Piano, Harpsichord, Clavi
9	Novelty	Melodic Percussion, Wah Trumpet, Synth, Whistle, Kazoo, Perc. Organ
10	Bellows	Accordion, French Accordion, Mussette, Harmonica, Pump Organ, Bagpipes

Ain't No Sunshine

Registration 8
Rhythm: 8-Beat or Blues

Words and Music by
Bill Withers

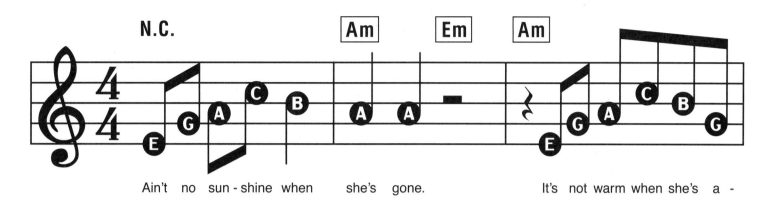

Ain't no sun - shine when she's gone. It's not warm when she's a -

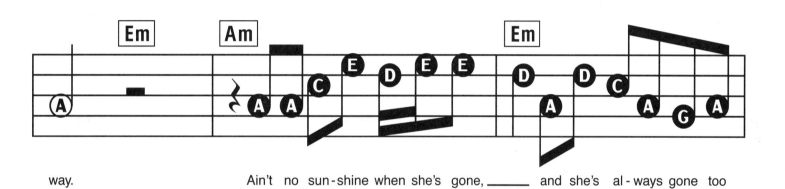

way. Ain't no sun - shine when she's gone, _____ and she's al - ways gone too

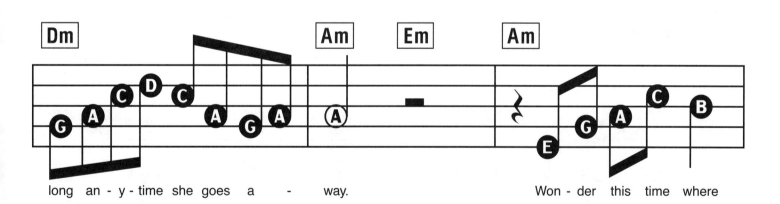

long an - y - time she goes a - way. Won - der this time where

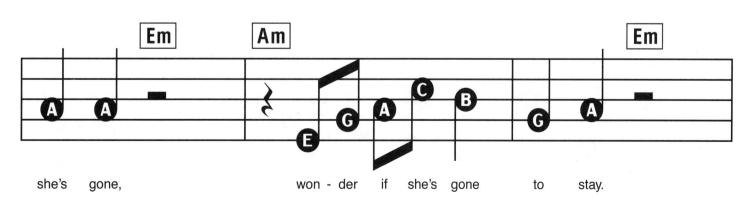

she's gone, won - der if she's gone to stay.

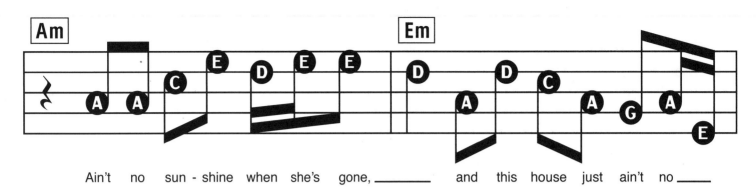

Ain't no sun - shine when she's gone, _____ and this house just ain't no _____

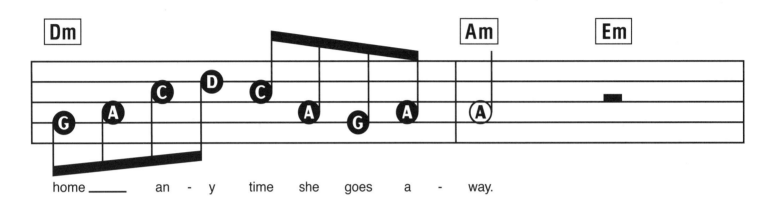

home _____ an - y time she goes a - way.

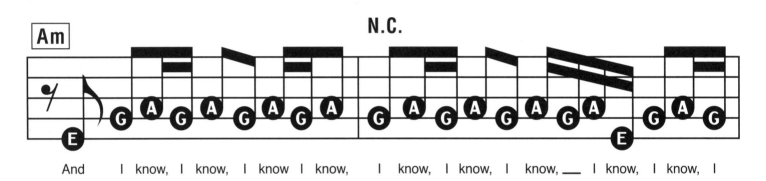

And I know, I know, I know I know, I know, I know, I know, _____ I know, I know, I

know, I know, I know, _____ I know, I know, I know, I know I know, I know, I know, I know,

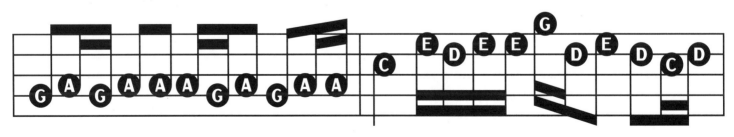

I know, I know, I know I know, I know, I know, hey, I ought to leave the young thing a - lone, _____

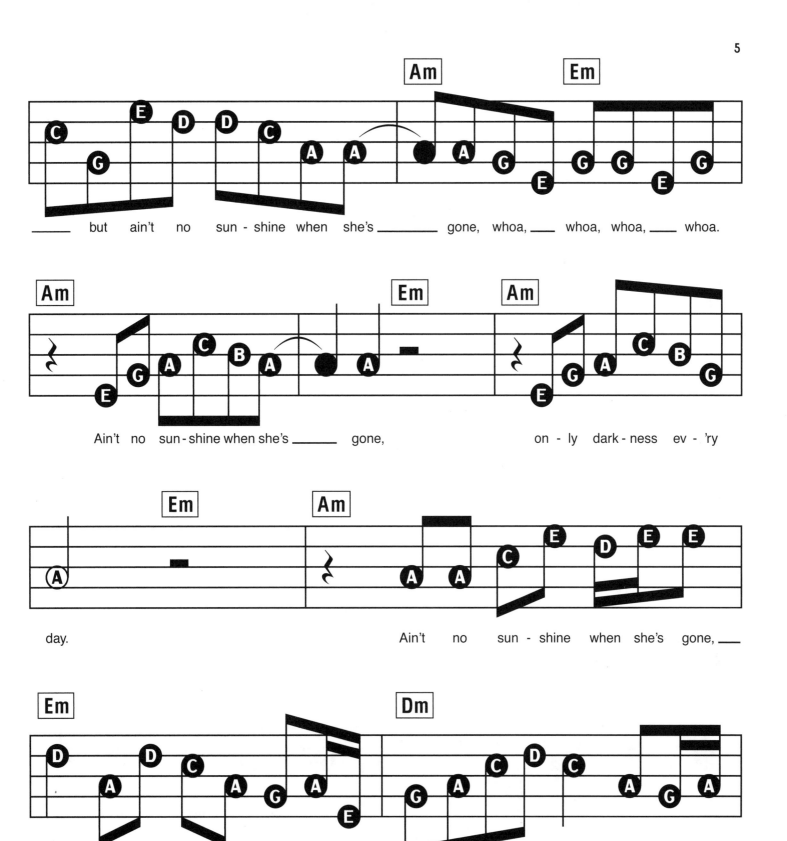

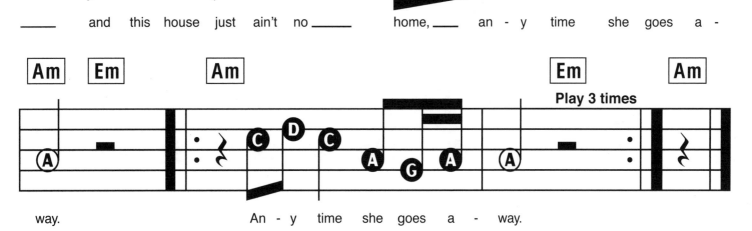

All About That Bass

Registration 2
Rhythm: Pop or Rock

Words and Music by Kevin Kadish
and Meghan Trainor

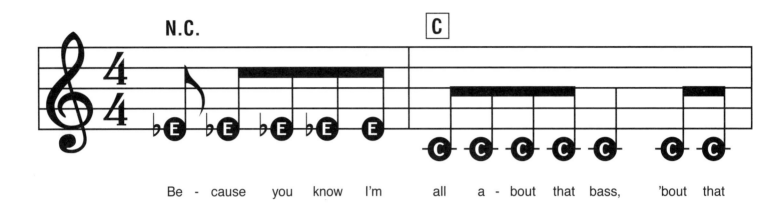

Be - cause you know I'm all a - bout that bass, 'bout that

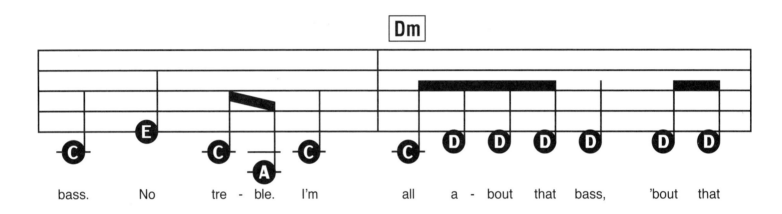

bass. No tre - ble. I'm all a - bout that bass, 'bout that

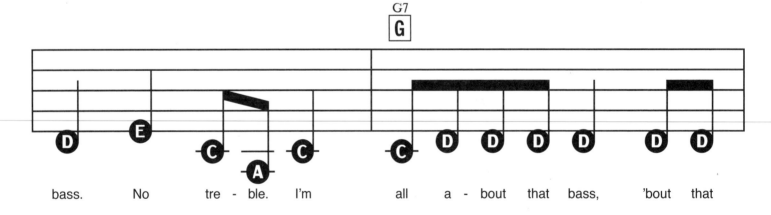

bass. No tre - ble. I'm all a - bout that bass, 'bout that

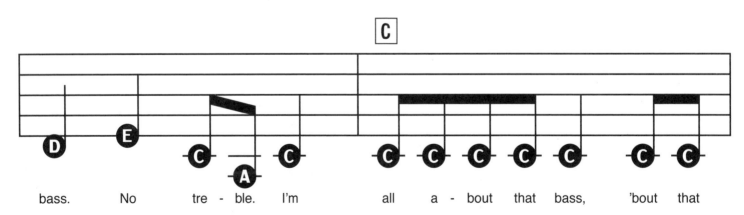

bass. No tre - ble. I'm all a - bout that bass, 'bout that

N.C.

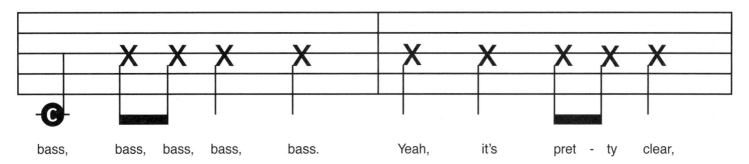

bass,   bass, bass, bass,   bass.   Yeah,   it's   pret - ty   clear,

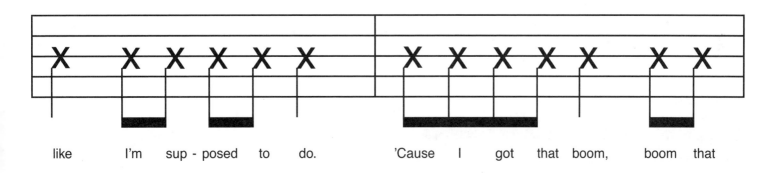

I   ain't   no   size   two.   But   I   can   shake   it,   shake   it

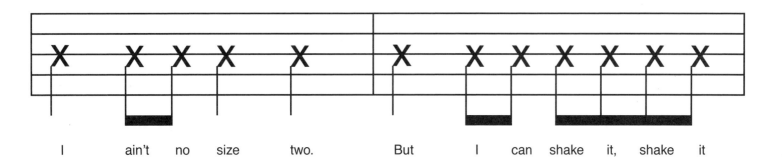

like   I'm   sup - posed   to   do.   'Cause   I   got   that   boom,   boom   that

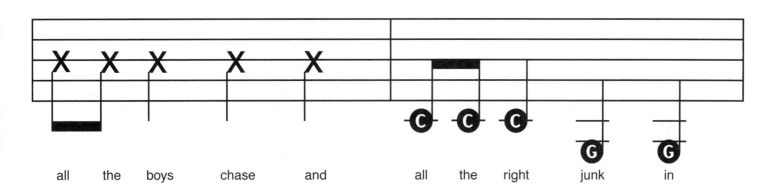

all   the   boys   chase   and   all   the   right   junk   in

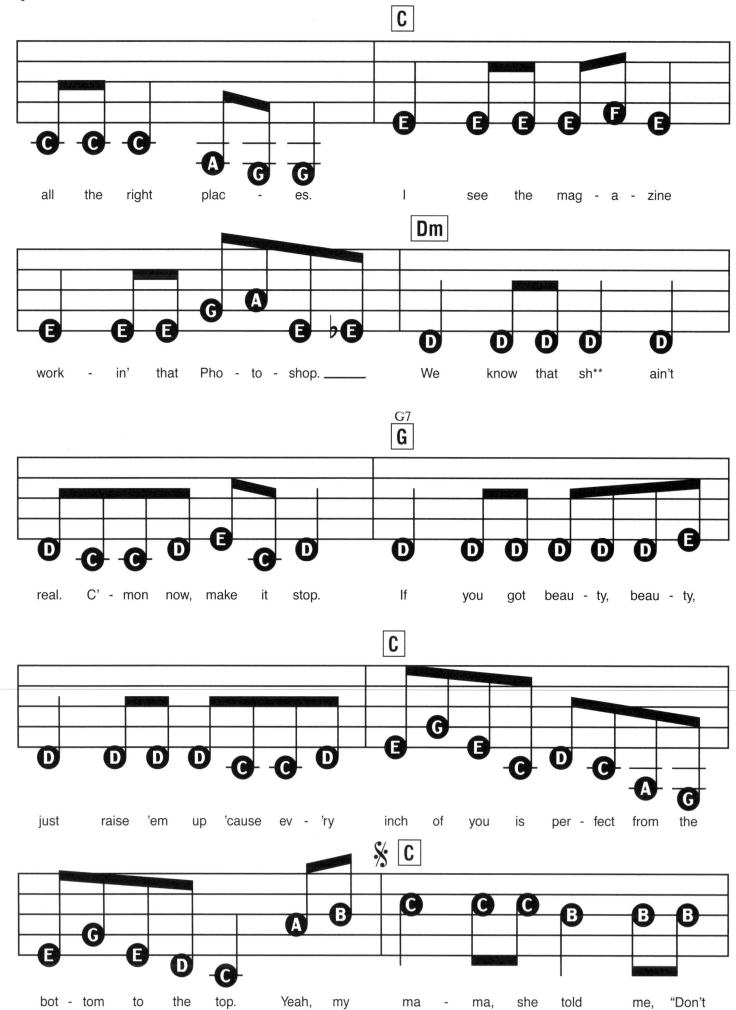

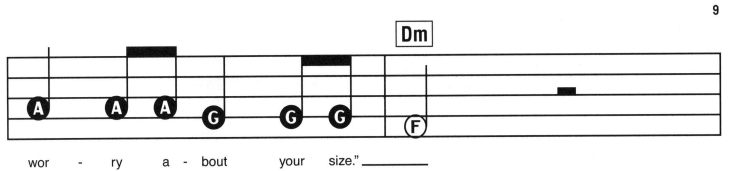

wor - ry a - bout your size." _____

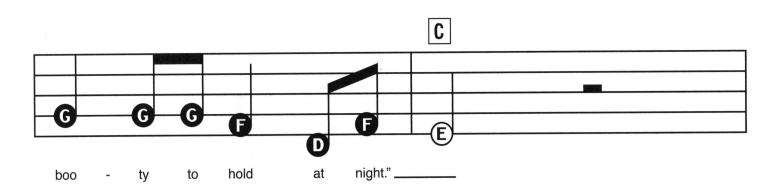

She says, "Boys like a lit - tle more

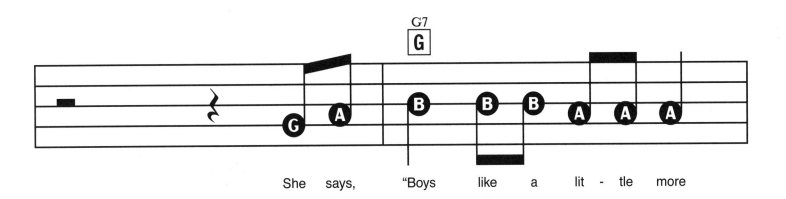

boo - ty to hold at night." _____

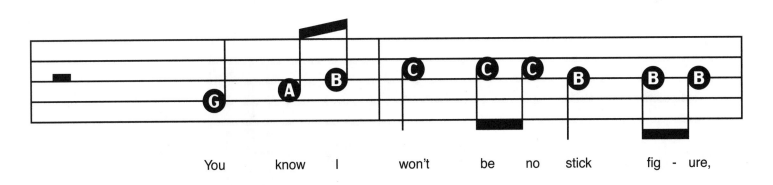

You know I won't be no stick fig - ure,

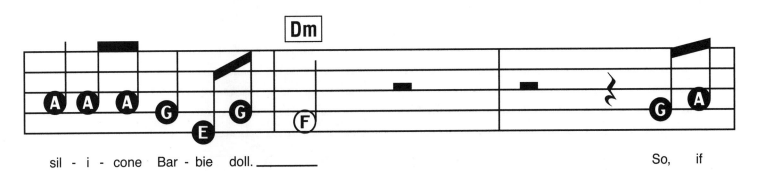

sil - i - cone Bar - bie doll. _____ So, if

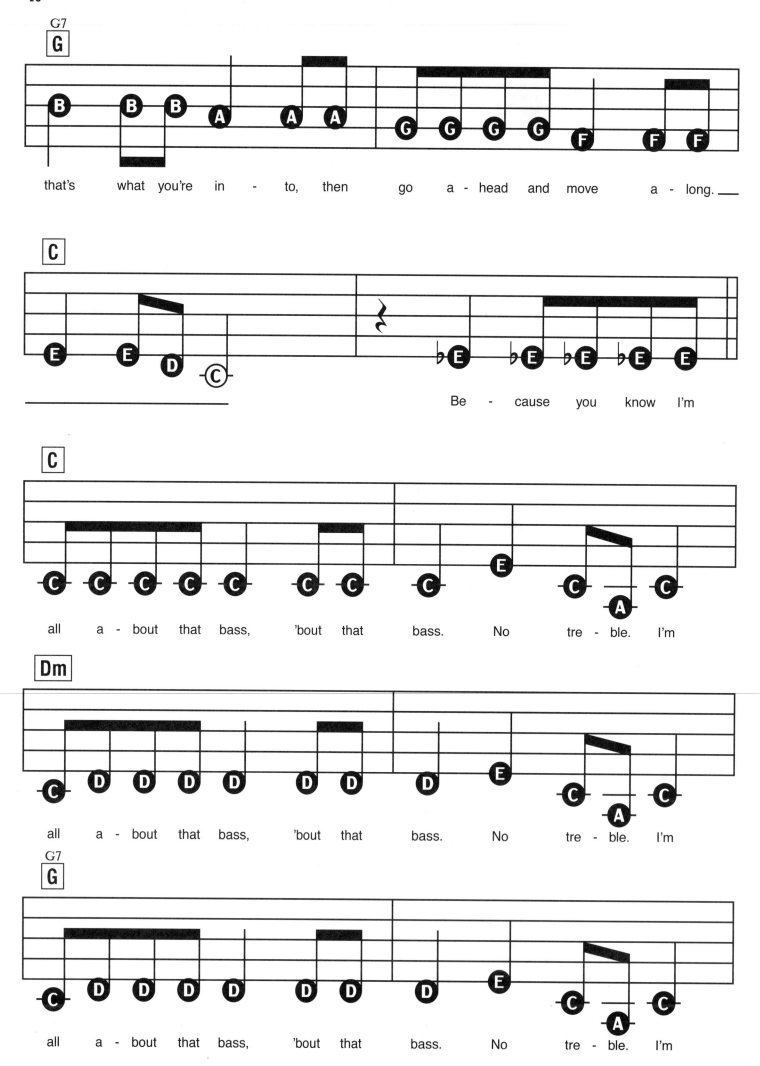

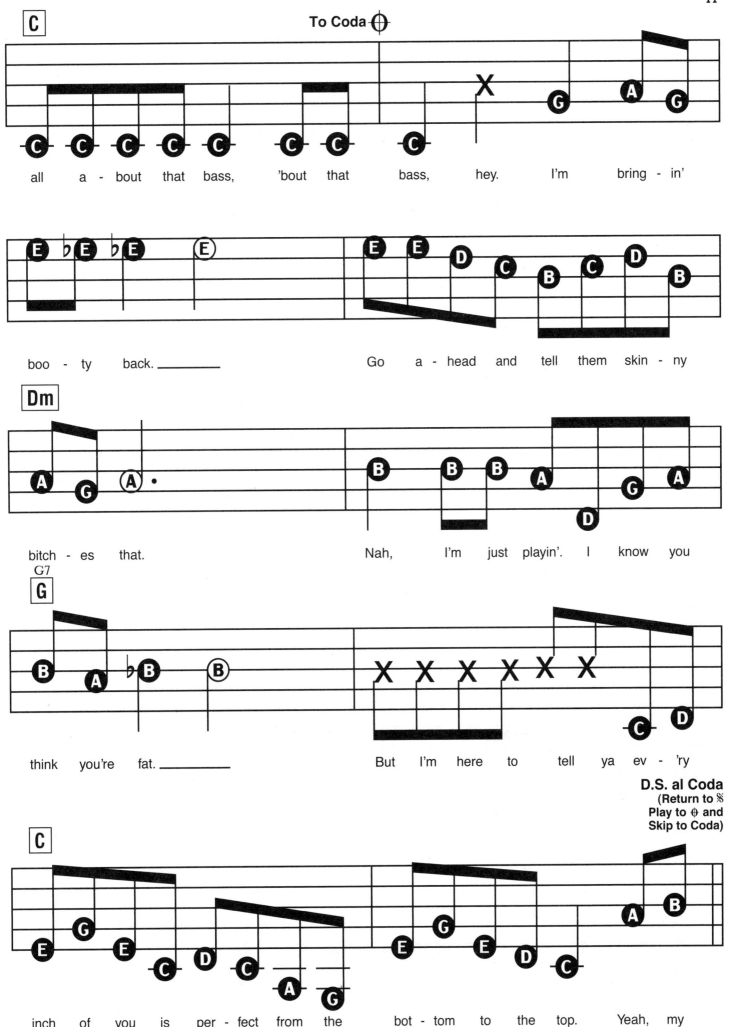

12

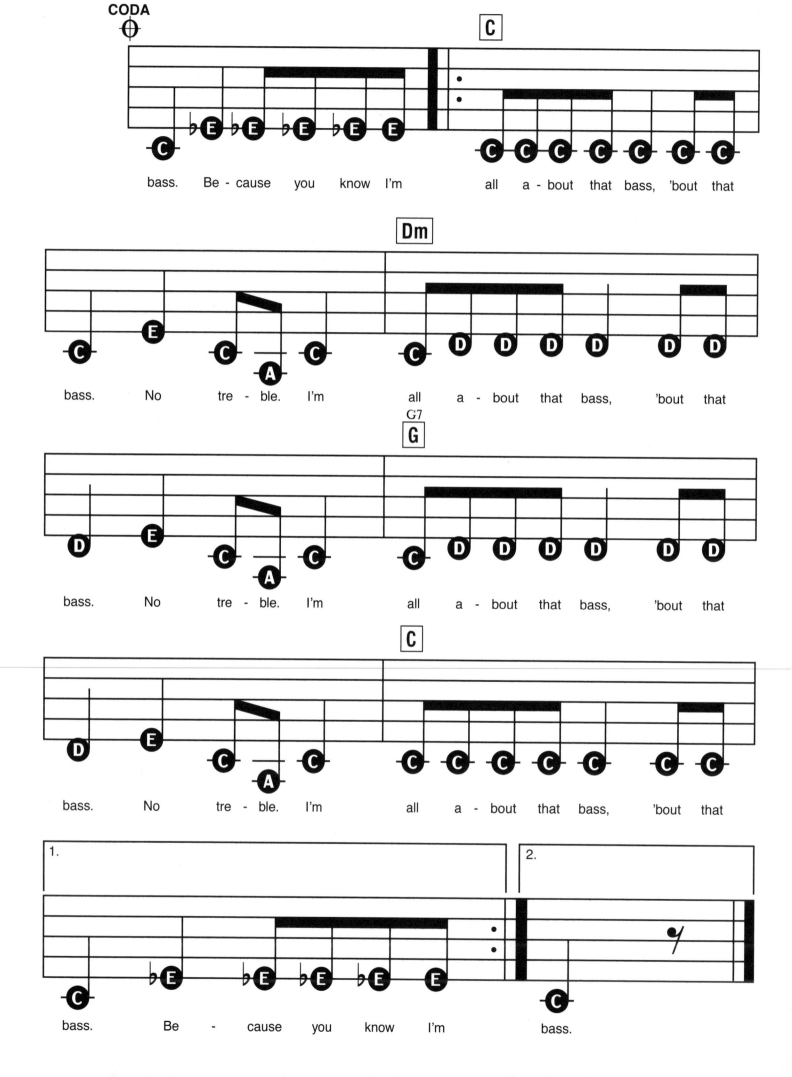

Chasing Cars

Registration 8
Rhythm: Rock or Techno

Words and Music by Gary Lightbody,
Tom Simpson, Paul Wilson,
Jonathan Quinn and Nathan Connolly

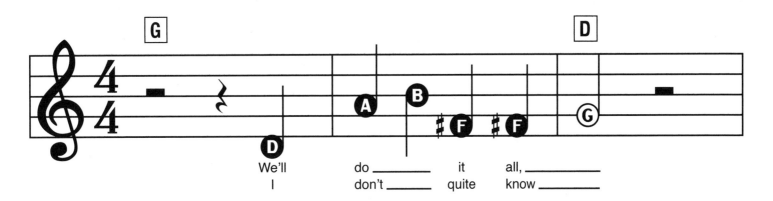

We'll do it all,
I don't quite know

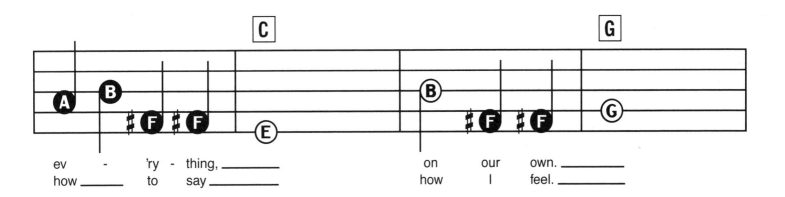

ev - 'ry - thing,   on our own.
how to say   how I feel.

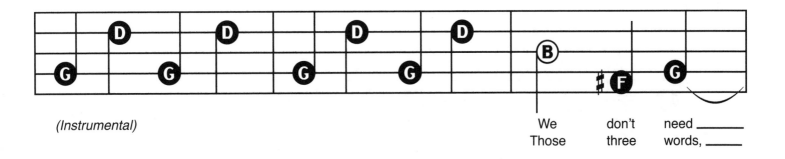

(Instrumental)

We don't need
Those three words,

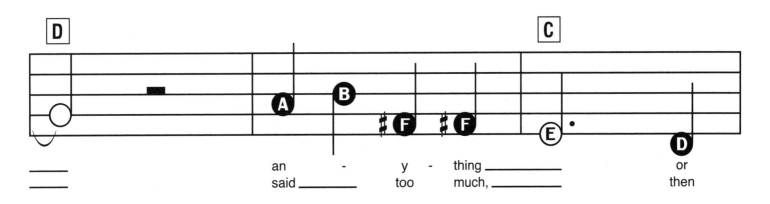

an - y - thing or
said too much, then

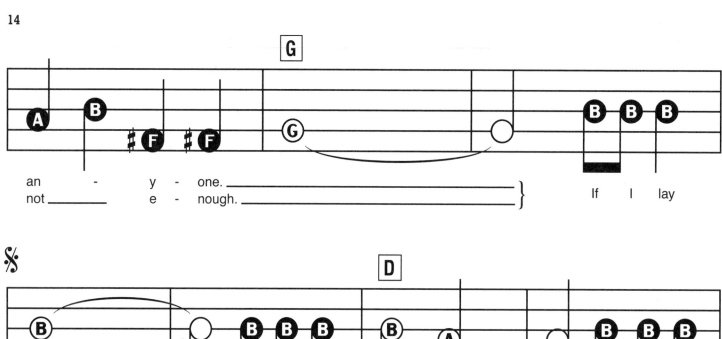

an - y - one. _____
not _____ e - nough. _____

If I lay

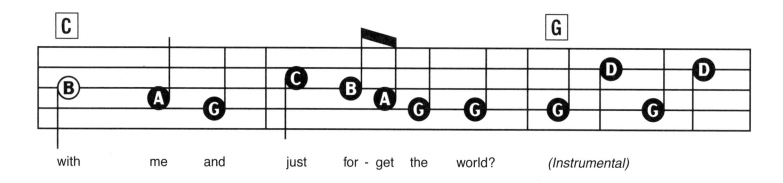

here, _____ if I just lay here, _____ would you lie

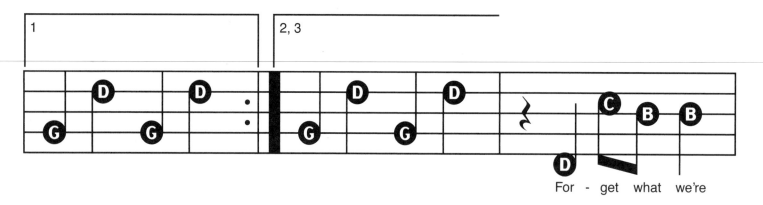

with me and just for - get the world? *(Instrumental)*

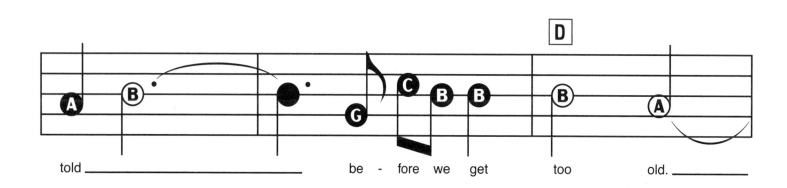

For - get what we're

told _____ be - fore we get too old. _____

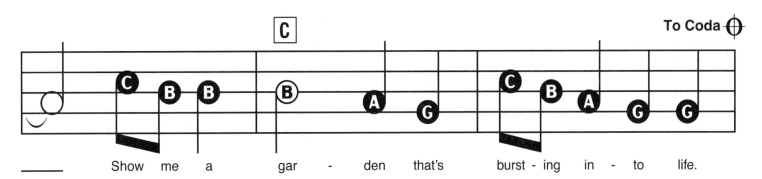

To Coda ⊕

Show me a gar - den that's burst-ing in - to life.

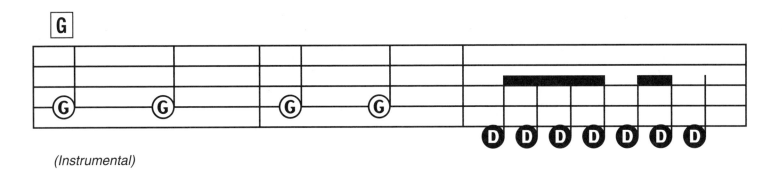

(Instrumental)

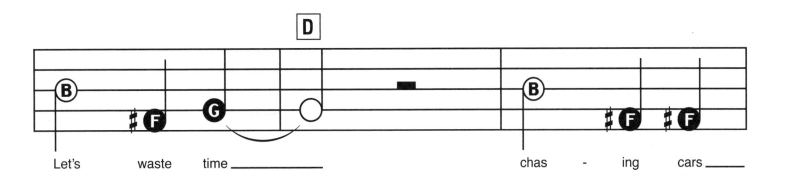

Let's waste time _____ chas - ing cars _____

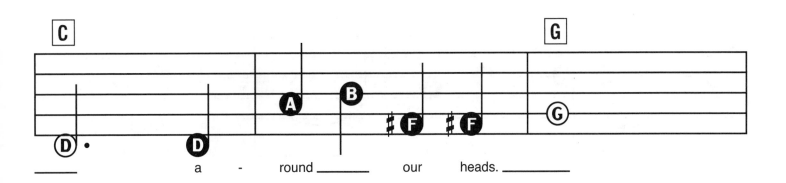

_____ a - round _____ our heads. _____

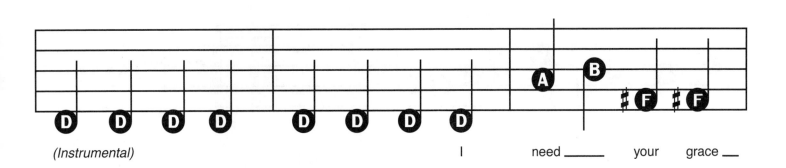

(Instrumental) I need _____ your grace _

16

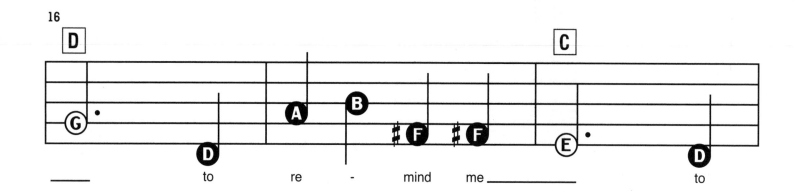

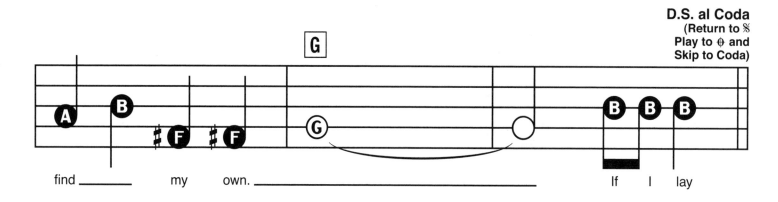

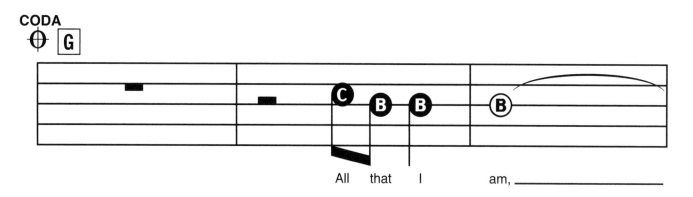

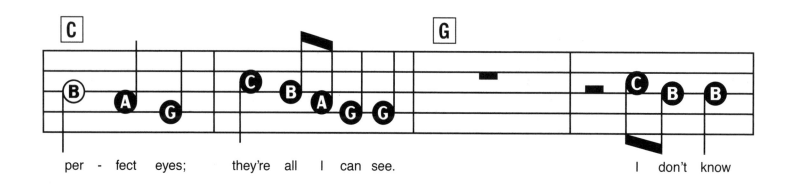

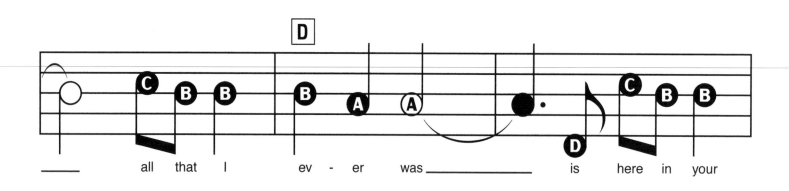

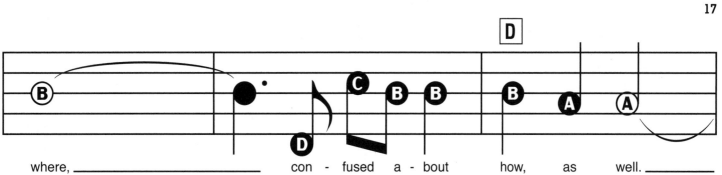

where, _____ con - fused a - bout how, as well. _____

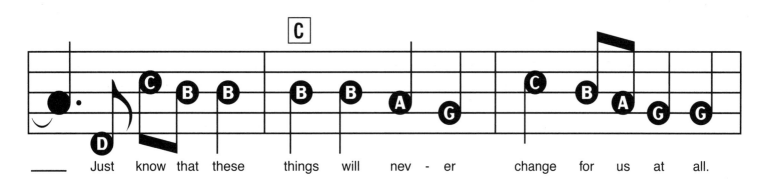

____ Just know that these things will nev - er change for us at all.

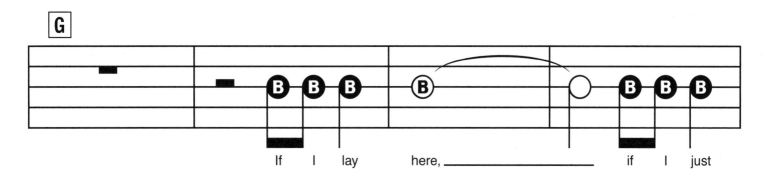

If I lay here, _____ if I just

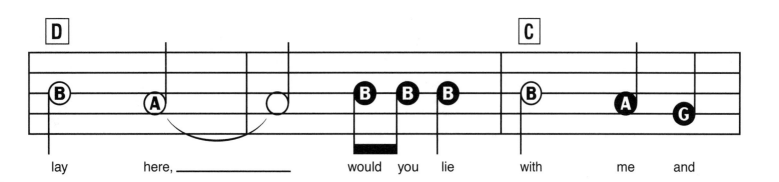

lay here, _____ would you lie with me and

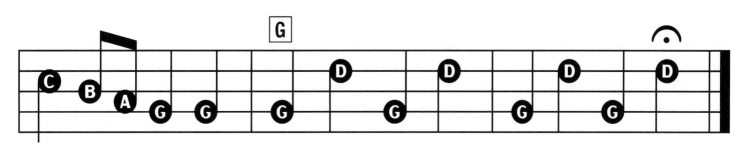

just for - get the world? *(Instrumental)*

All Along the Watchtower

Registration 4
Rhythm: Rock

Words and Music by
Bob Dylan

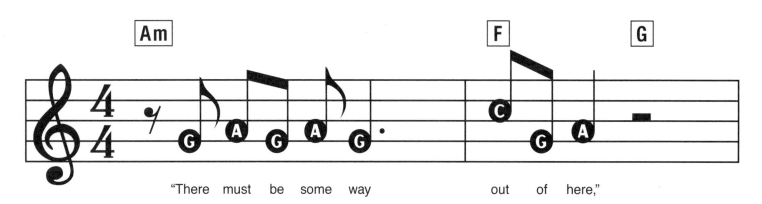

"There must be some way out of here,"

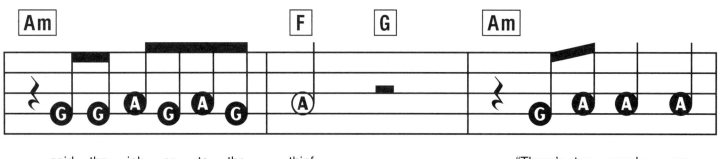

said the jok - er to the thief. "There's too much con -

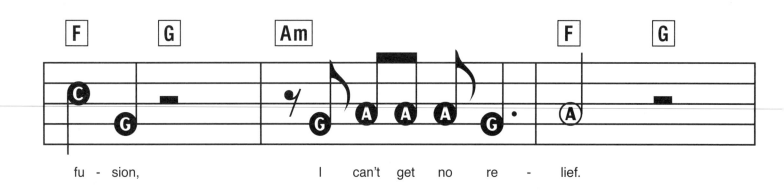

fu - sion, I can't get no re - lief.

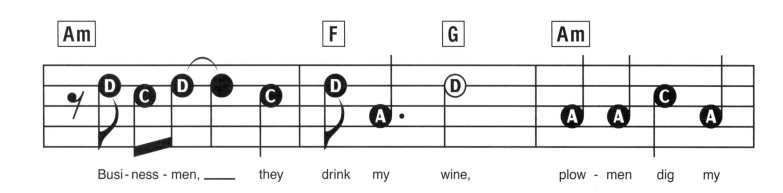

Busi - ness - men, _____ they drink my wine, plow - men dig my

earth.   None of them a - long the line _____

know what an - y of it is   worth."

"No rea - son to get ex - cit - ed,"

the thief, he kind - ly   spoke. ___

"There are man - y here a - mong   us

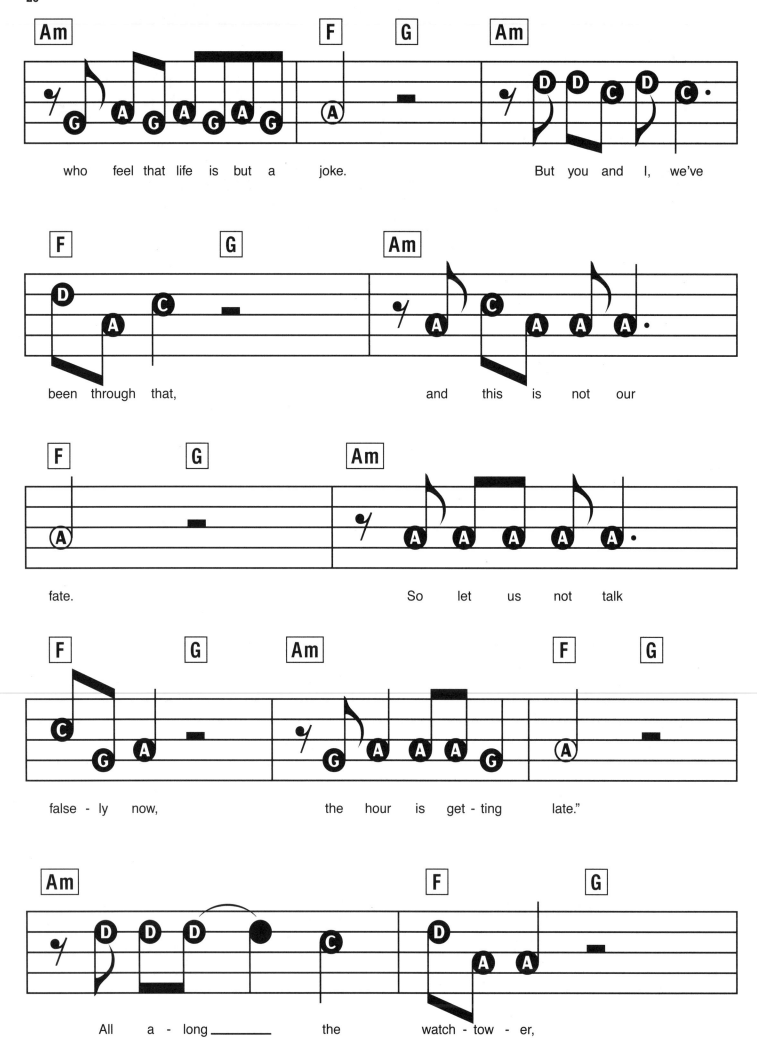

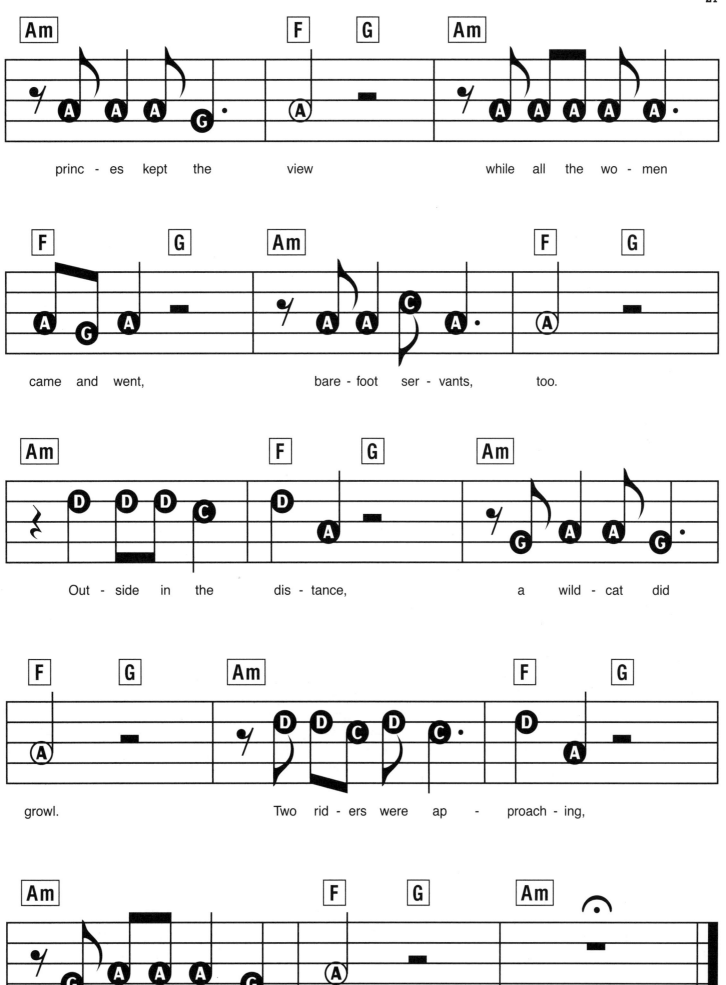

Call Me the Breeze

Registration 4
Rhythm: Country Swing

Words and Music by
John Cale

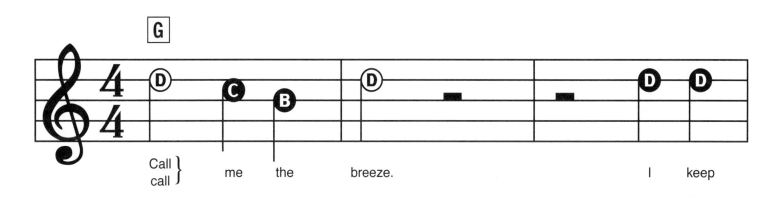

Call } me the breeze.   I keep
call }

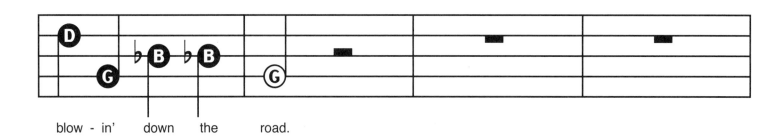

blow - in' down the road.

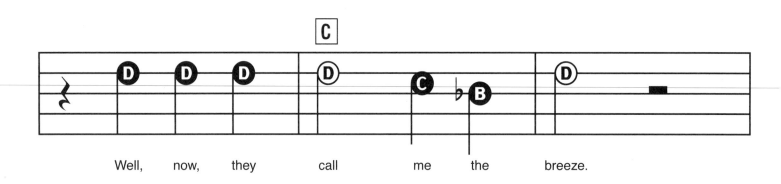

Well, now, they call me the breeze.

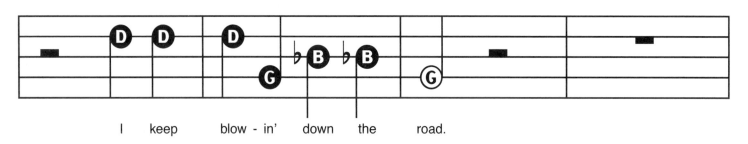

I keep blow - in' down the road.

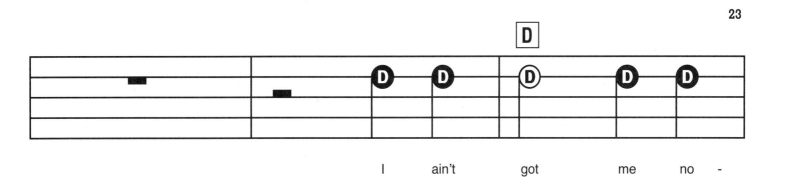

I ain't got me no -

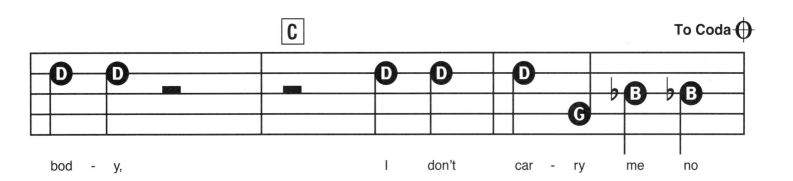

bod - y,   I   don't   car - ry   me   no

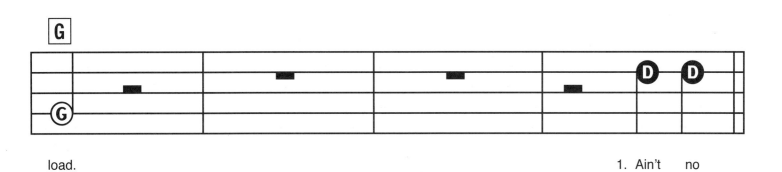

load.   1. Ain't   no

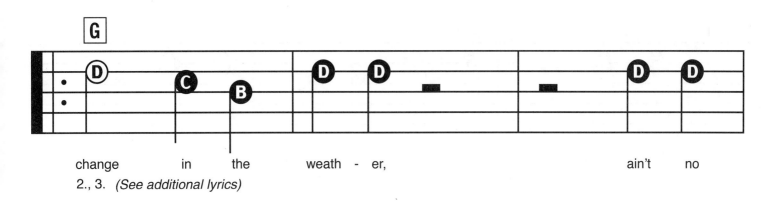

change   in   the   weath - er,   ain't   no

2., 3. *(See additional lyrics)*

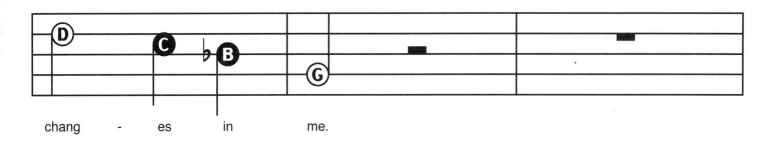

chang - es   in   me.

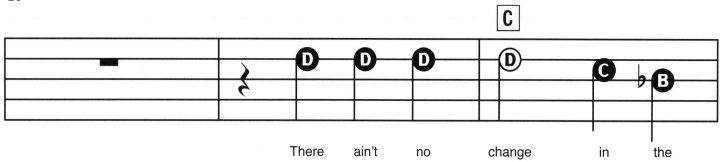

There ain't no change in the

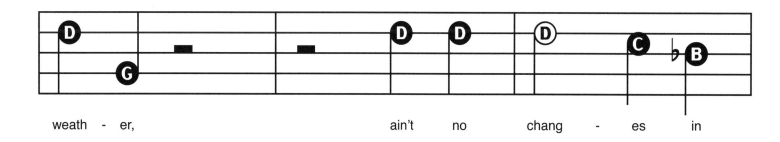

weath - er, ain't no chang - es in

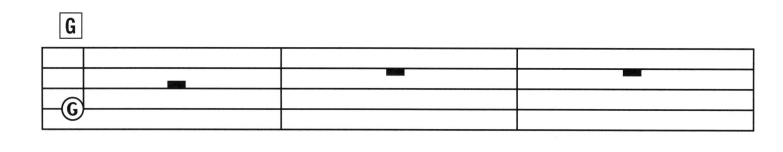

me.

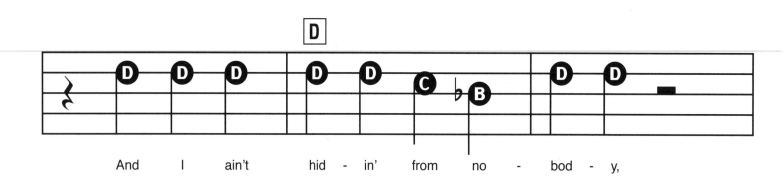

And I ain't hid - in' from no - bod - y,

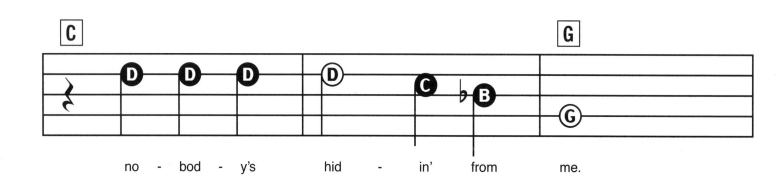

no - bod - y's hid - in' from me.

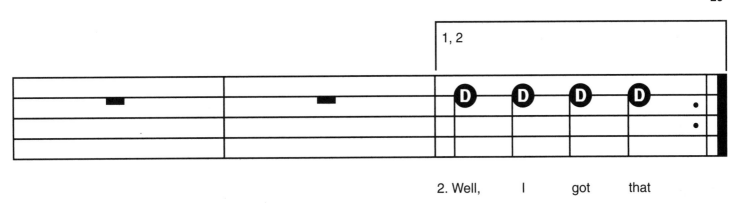

2. Well   I   got   that

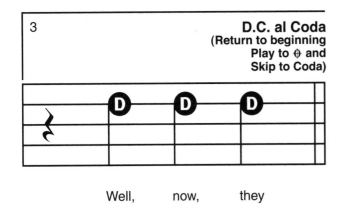

Well,   now,   they

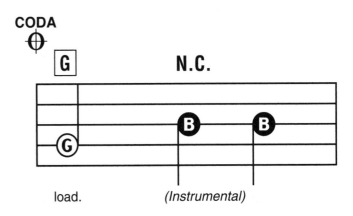

load.   (Instrumental)

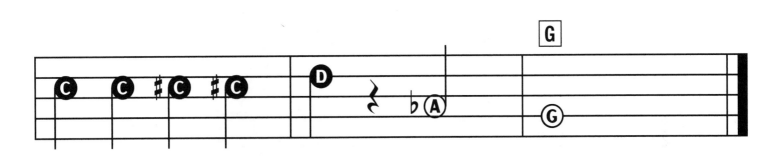

Additional Lyrics

2. Well, I got that green light, baby, I got to keep movin' on.
   Well, I got that green light, baby, I got to keep movin' on.
   Well, I might go out to California, might go down to Georgia, I don't know.

3. Well, I dig you Georgia peaches, makes me feel right at home.
   Well, now, I dig you Georgia peaches, makes me feel right at home.
   But I don't love me no one woman, so I can't stay in Georgia long.

Closer to Free

Registration 4
Rhythm: 8-Beat or Rock

Words and Music by Sam Llanas
and Kurt Neumann

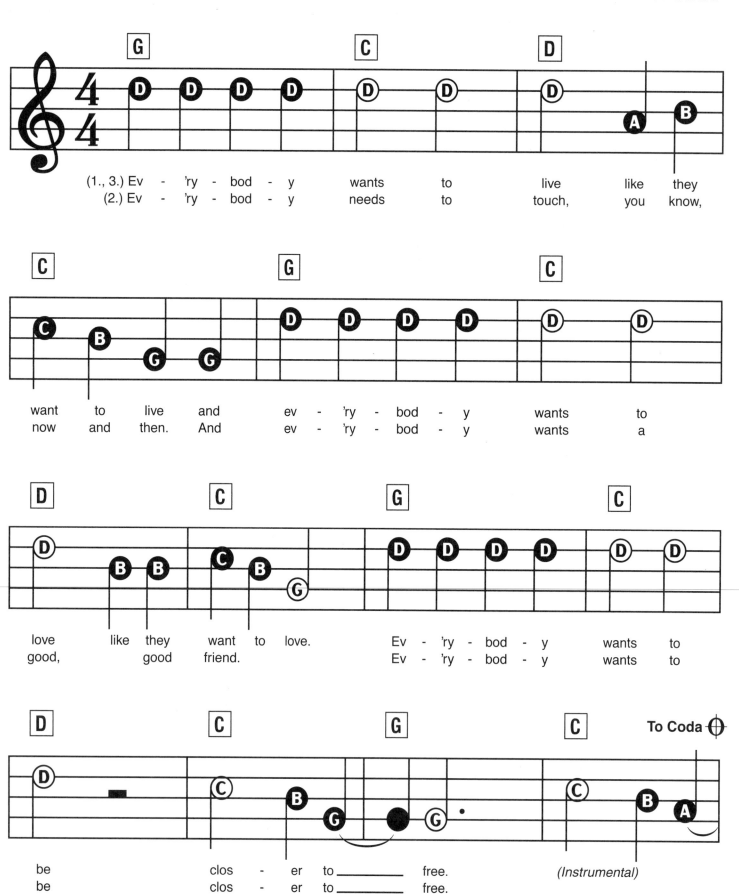

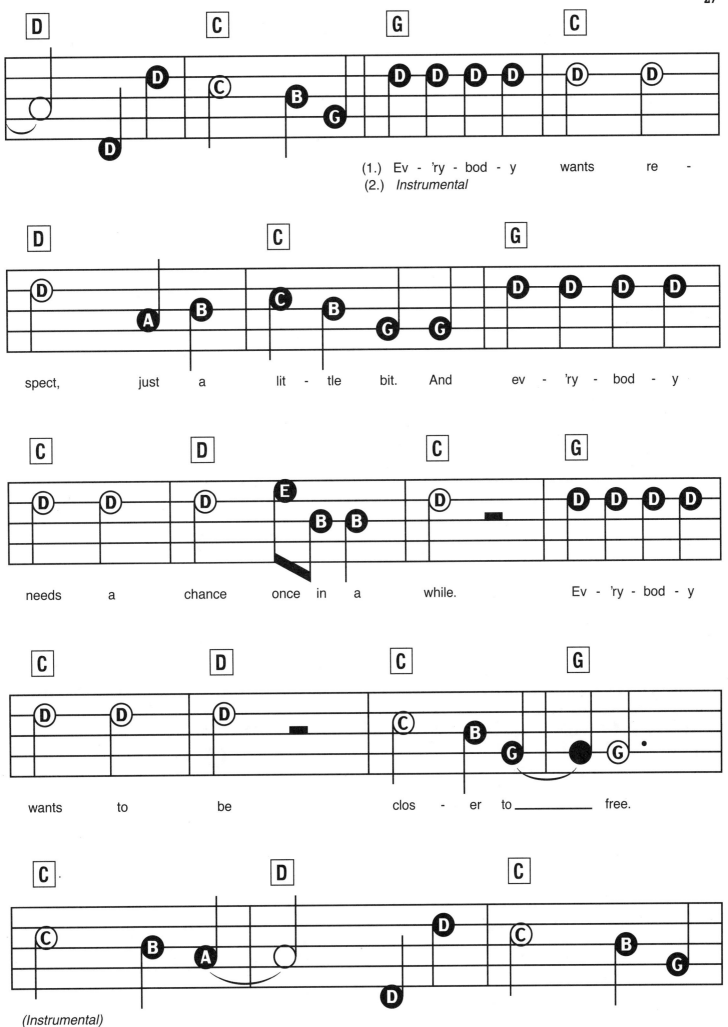

28

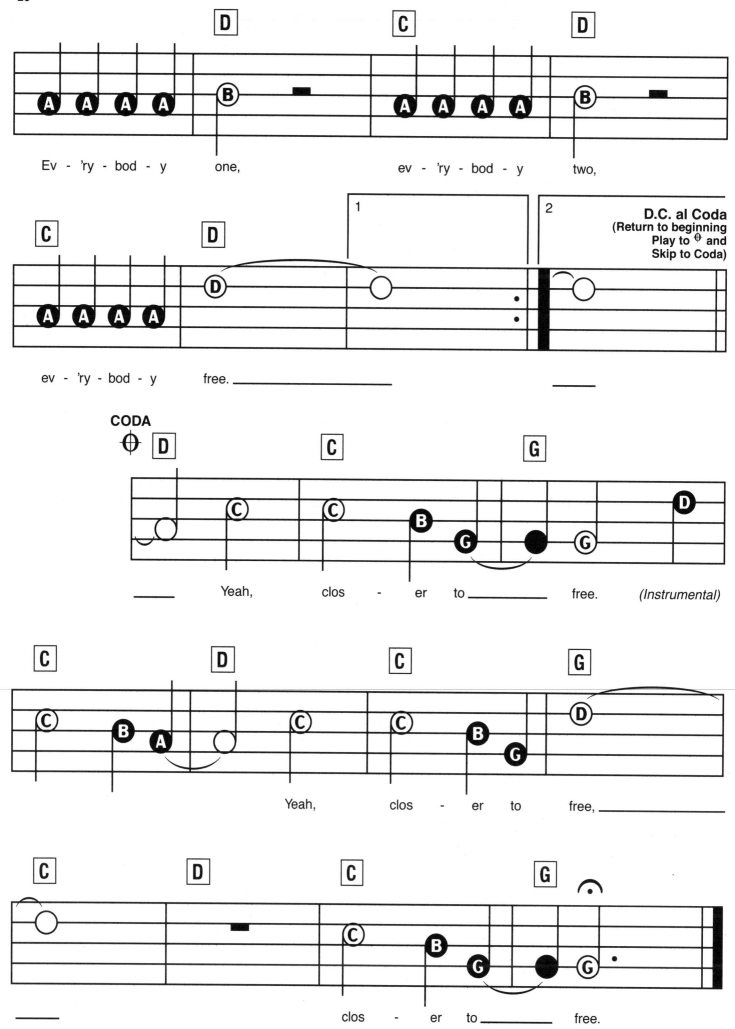

Hang On Sloopy

Registration 2
Rhythm: Rock

Words and Music by Wes Farrell
and Bert Russell

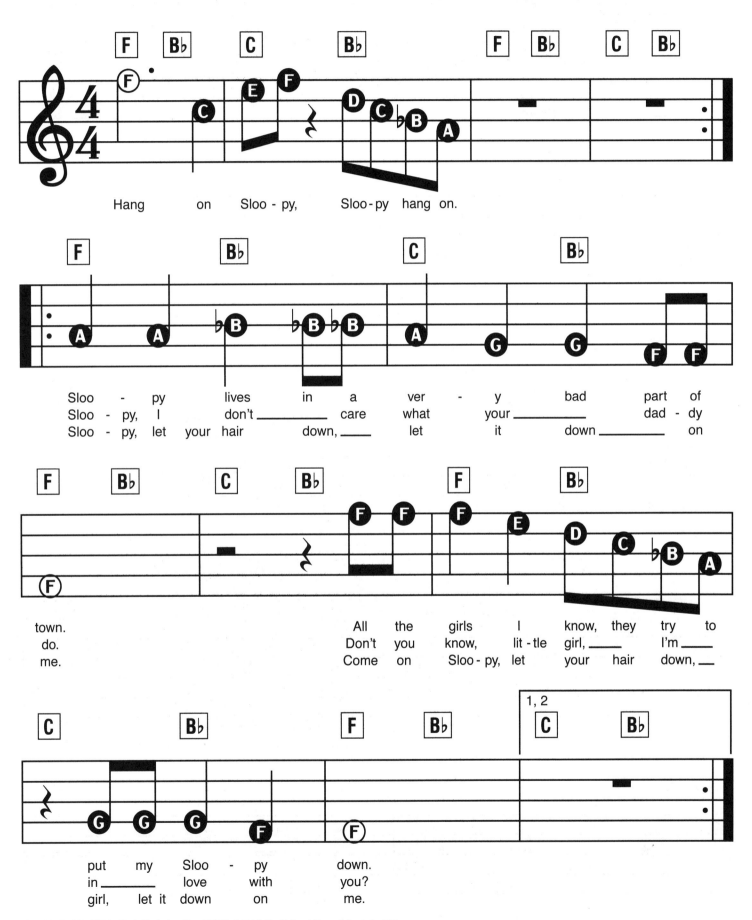

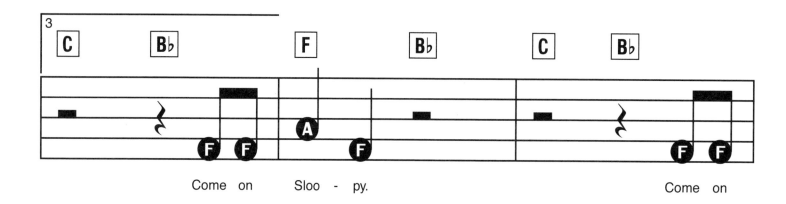

Come on   Sloo - py.   Come on

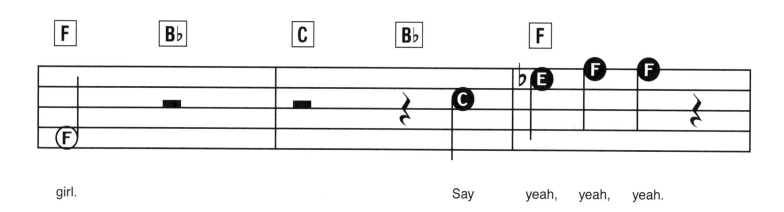

girl.   Say   yeah,   yeah,   yeah.

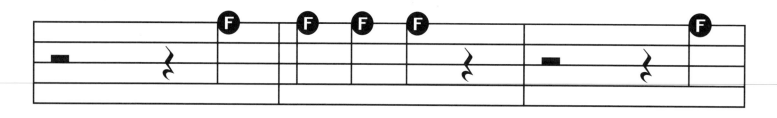

Good,   good,   good,   good.   Good,

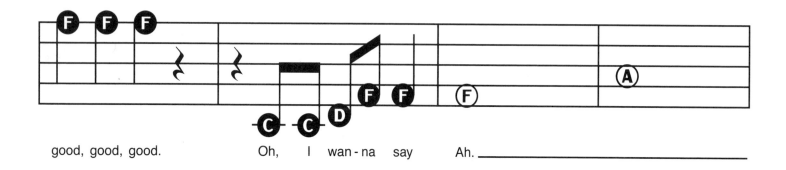

good, good, good.   Oh,   I   wan - na   say   Ah. _____

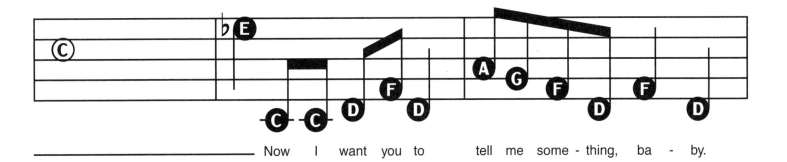

Now I want you to tell me some - thing, ba - by.

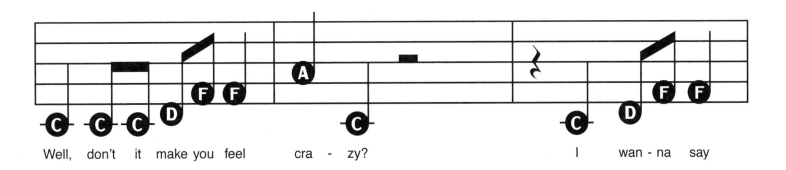

Well, don't it make you feel cra - zy? I wan - na say

Ah.

Repeat and Fade

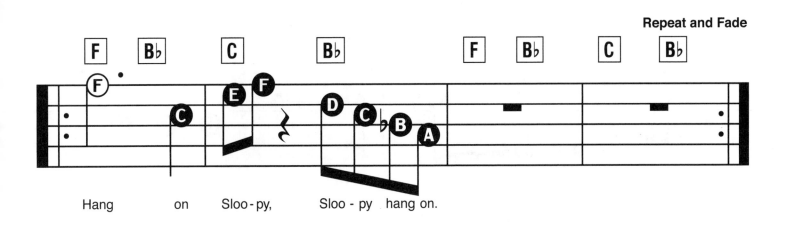

Hang on Sloo - py, Sloo - py hang on.

Evil Ways

Registration 2
Rhythm: Rock or Pop

Words and Music by
Sonny Henry

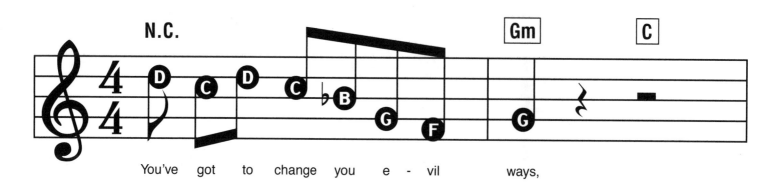

You've got to change you e - vil ways,

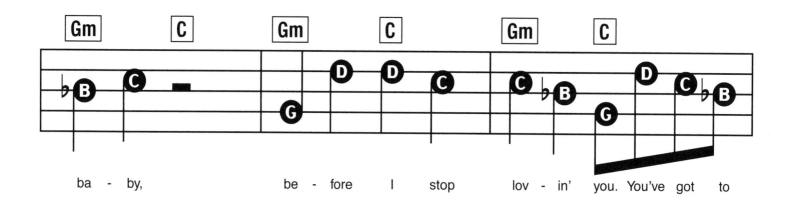

ba - by, be - fore I stop lov - in' you. You've got to

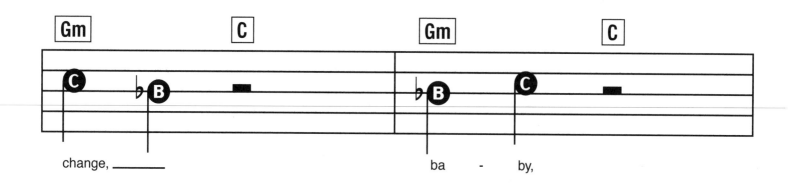

change, _____ ba - by,

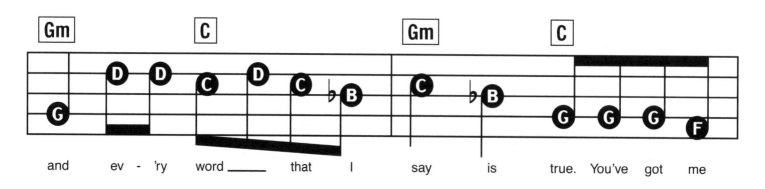

and ev - 'ry word _____ that I say is true. You've got me

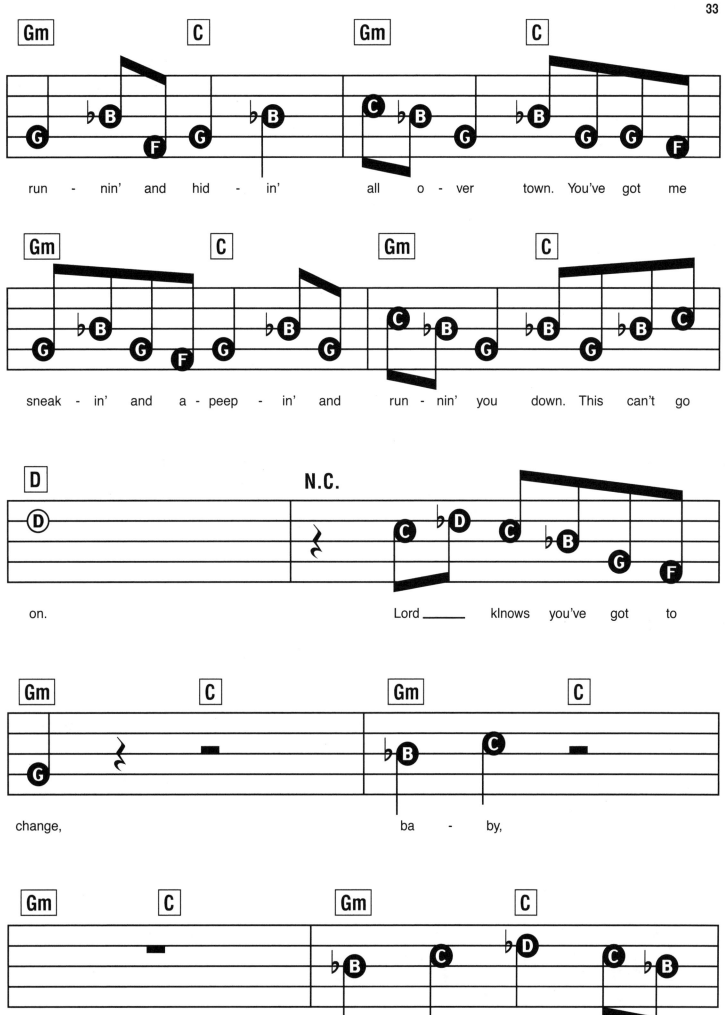

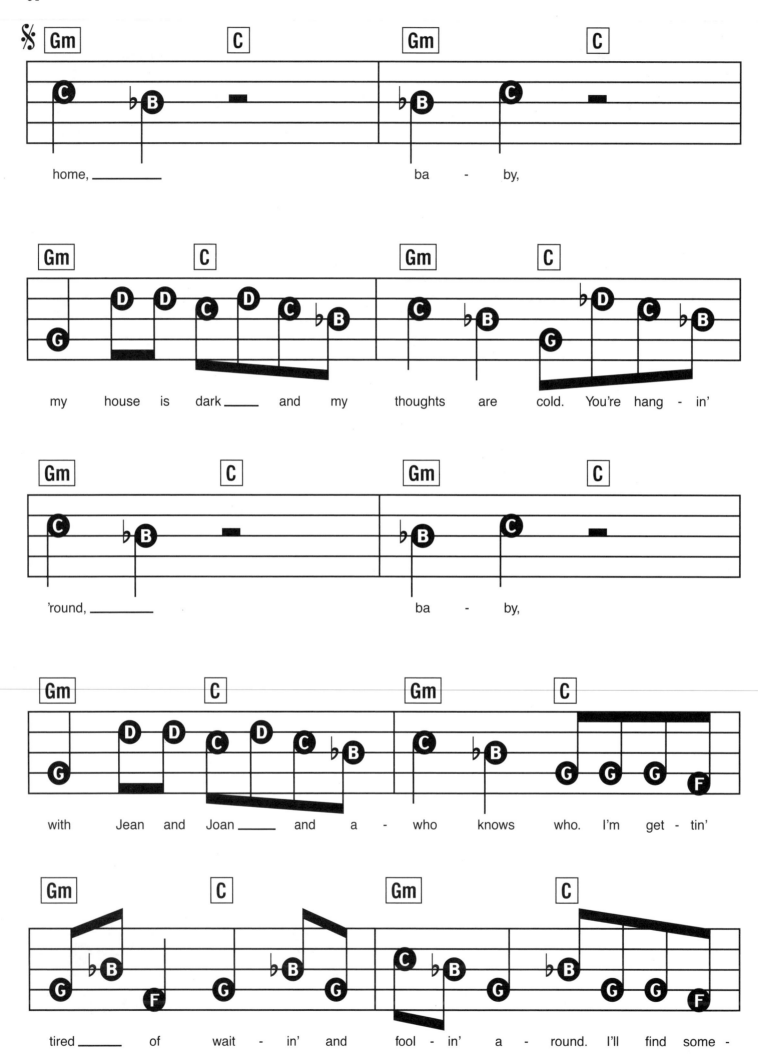

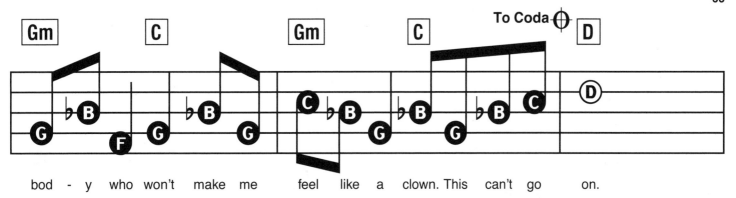

bod - y who won't make me feel like a clown. This can't go on.

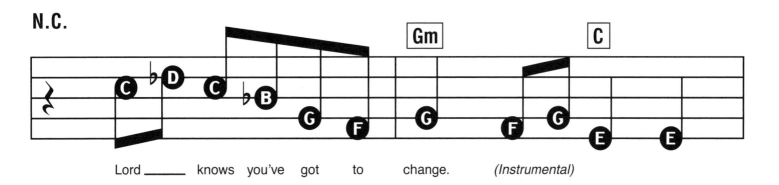

Lord _____ knows you've got to change. *(Instrumental)*

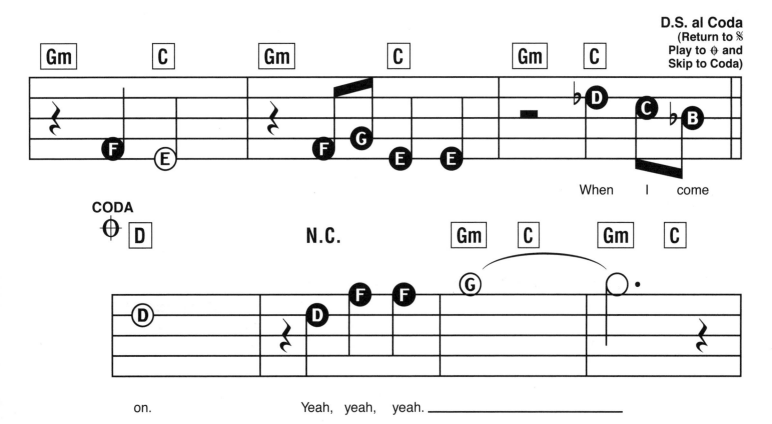

on. Yeah, yeah, yeah. _____

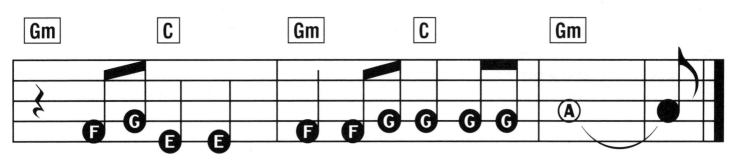

(Instrumental)

The First Cut Is the Deepest

Registration 2
Rhythm: 8-Beat, Pops or Rock

Words and Music by
Cat Stevens

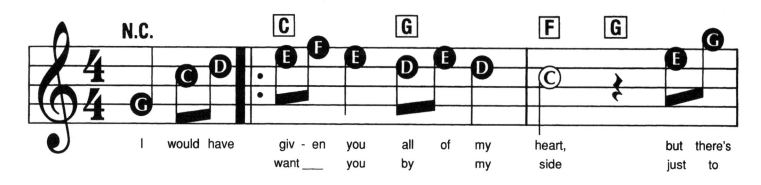

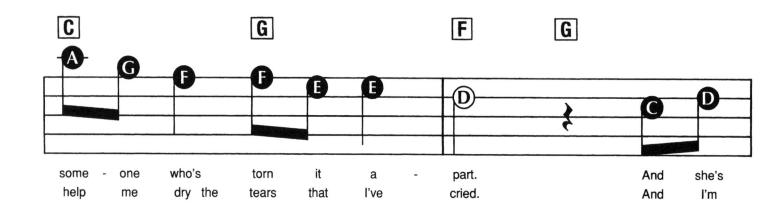

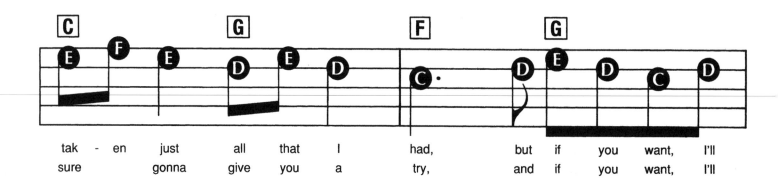

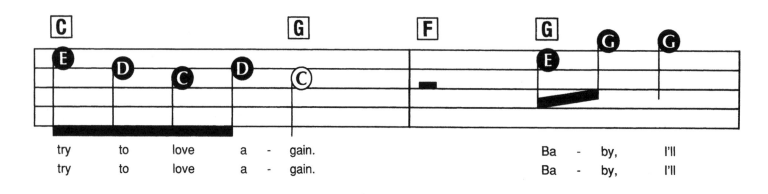

Folsom Prison Blues

Registration 3
Rhythm: Rock or Fox Trot

Words and Music by
John R. Cash

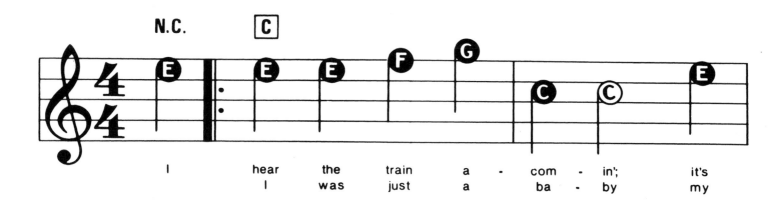

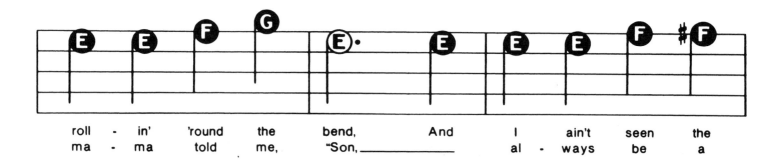

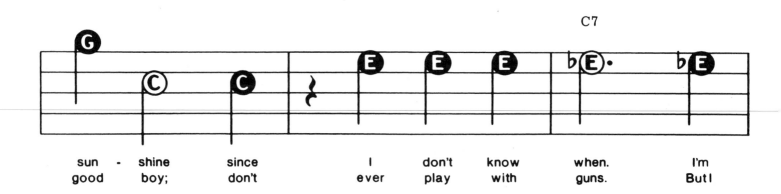

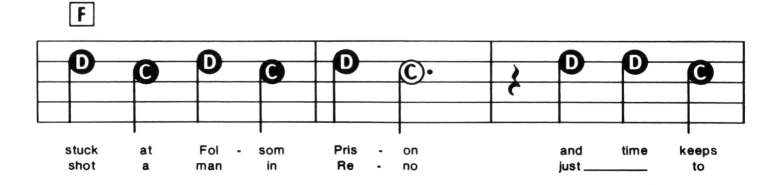

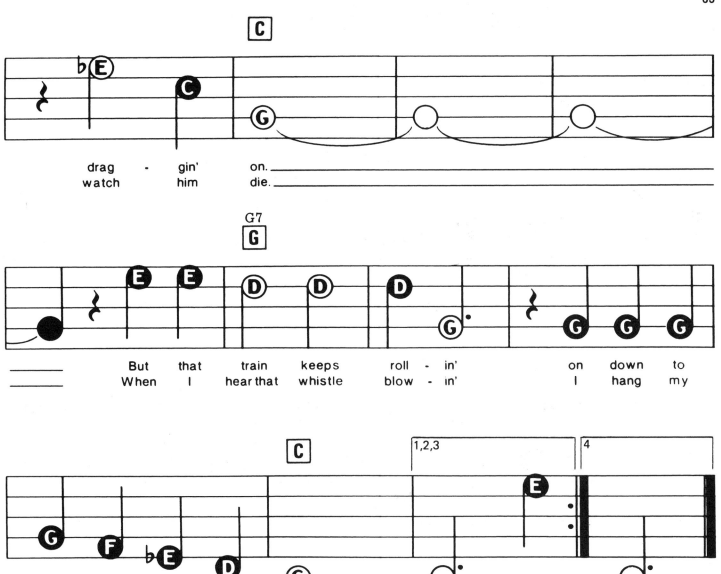

drag - gin' on. _____
watch him die. _____

But that train keeps roll - in' on down to
When I hear that whistle blow - in' I hang my

San _____ An - tone. _____
head _____ and _____ cry. _____

3. I bet there's rich folks eatin' in a fancy dining car.
   They're prob'ly drinkin' coffee and smokin' big cigars,
   But I know I had it comin', I know I can't be free,
   But those people keep a-movin', and that's what tortures me.

4. Well, if they freed me from this prison, if that railroad train was mine,
   I bet I'd move over a little farther down the line,
   Far from Folsom Prison, that's where I want to stay.
   And I'd let that lonesome whistle blow my blues away.

For What It's Worth

Registration 1
Rhythm: Rock or Slow Rock

Words and Music by
Stephen Stills

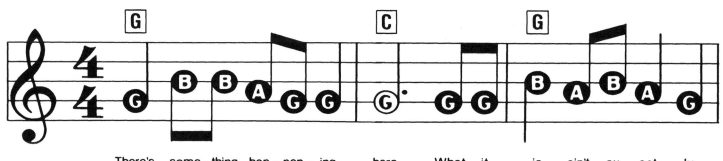

There's some-thing hap-pen-ing here, What it is ain't ex-act-ly

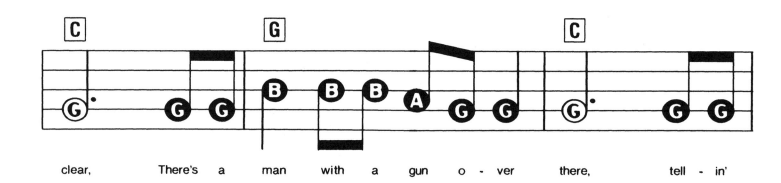

clear, There's a man with a gun o-ver there, tell-in'

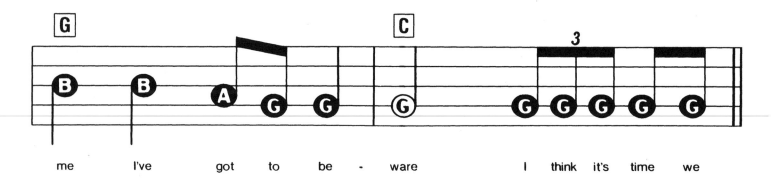

me I've got to be-ware I think it's time we

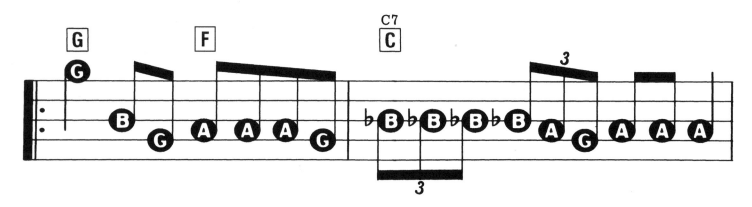

stop, chil-dren, what's that sound? ___ Ev-'ry-bod-y look what's go-in' down.

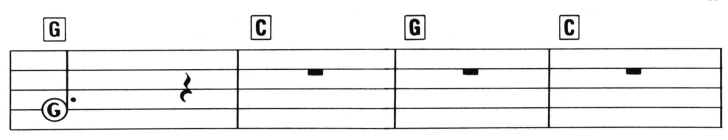

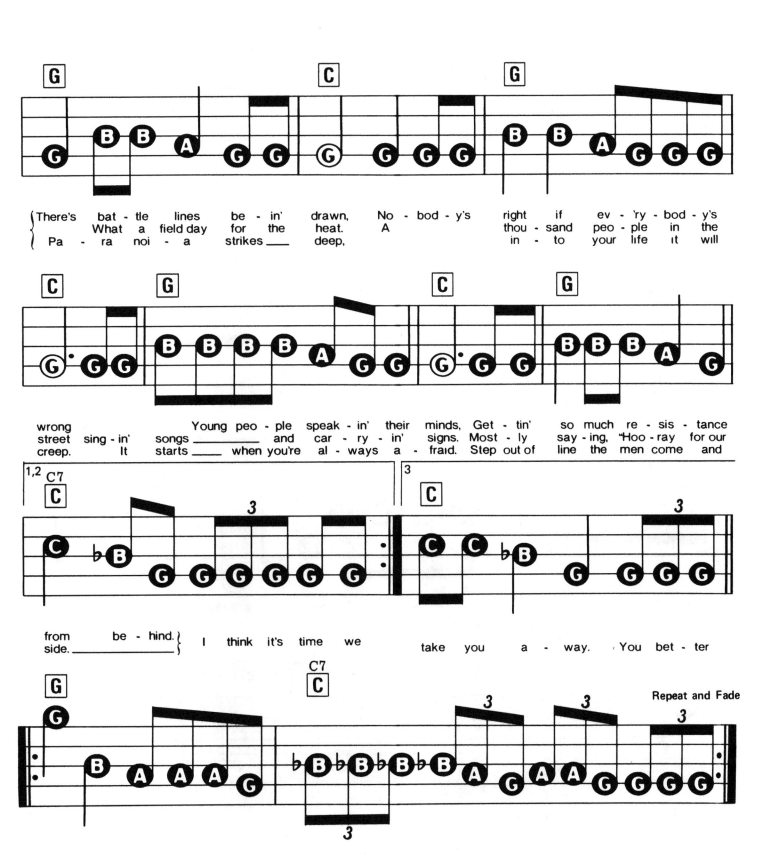

There's bat - tle lines be - in' drawn, No - bod - y's right if ev - 'ry - bod - y's
What a field day for the heat. A thou - sand peo - ple in the
Pa - ra noi - a strikes ___ deep, in - to your life it will

wrong Young peo - ple speak - in' their minds, Get - tin' so much re - sis - tance
street sing - in' songs ___ and car - ry - in' signs. Most - ly say - ing, "Hoo - ray for our
creep. It starts ___ when you're al - ways a - fraid. Step out of line the men come and

from be - hind. } I think it's time we take you a - way. You bet - ter
side. ___

stop, hey, what's that sound? ___ Ev - 'ry - bod - y look what's go - in' down. You bet - ter

Get Back

Registration 8
Rhythm: Rock

Words and Music by John Lennon
and Paul McCartney

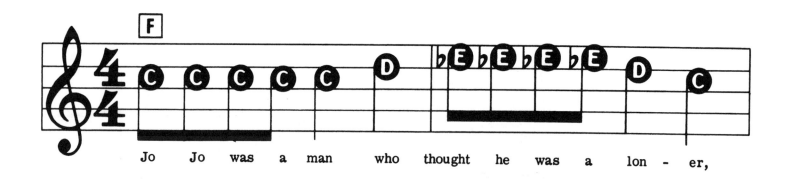

Jo Jo was a man who thought he was a lon - er,

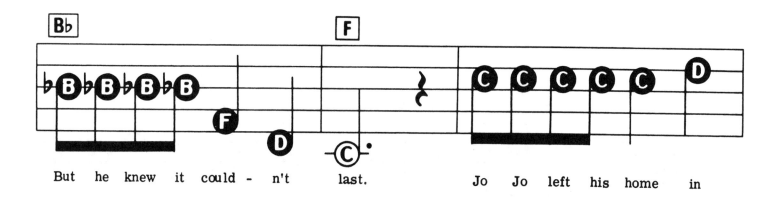

But he knew it could - n't last. Jo Jo left his home in

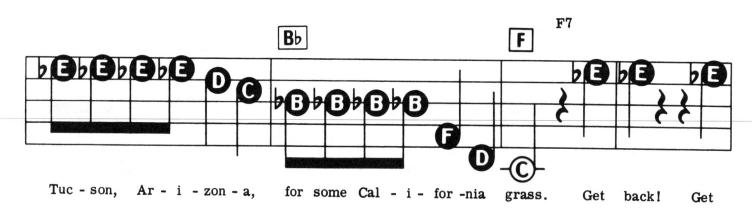

Tuc - son, Ar - i - zon - a, for some Cal - i - for - nia grass. Get back! Get

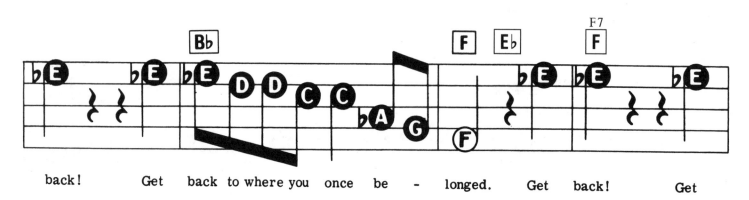

back! Get back to where you once be - longed. Get back! Get

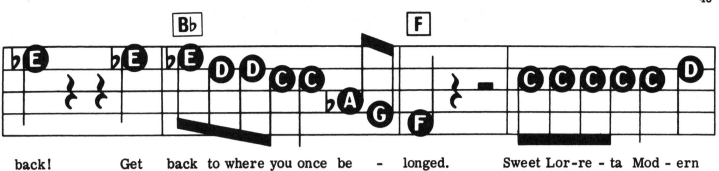

back!   Get   back to where you once be - longed.   Sweet Lor-re - ta Mod - ern

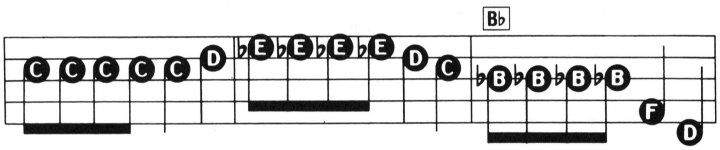

thought she was   a   wom - an,   but she was an - oth - er   man.

All   the girls a -round her say she's got   it   com - ing, But, she gets   it while she

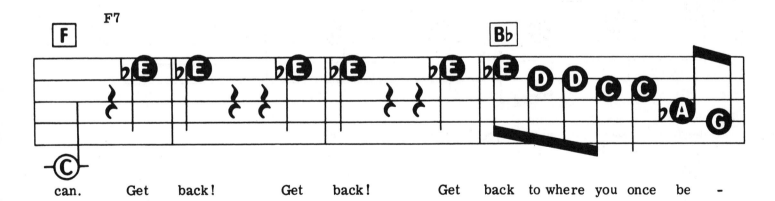

can.   Get   back!   Get   back!   Get   back to where you once be -

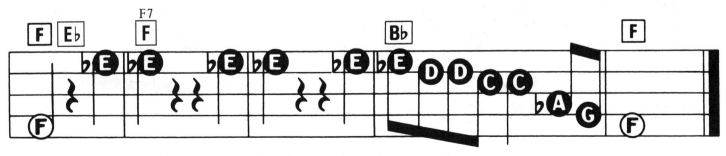

longed.   Get back!   Get back!   Get back to where you once be - longed.

Hold My Hand

Registration 7
Rhythm: 8-Beat or Rock

Words and Music by Darius Carlos Rucker, Everett Dean Felber,
Mark William Bryan and James George Sonefeld

With a lit - tle love
day
wast - ed

and some ten - der - ness ___ we'll
I saw you stand - ing there. ___ Your
and I was wast - ing time ___ 'til

walk up - on the wa - ter, we'll
head was down, your eyes were red, no
I thought a - bout your prob - lem, I

rise a - bove the mess. ___
comb had touched your hair. ___
thought a - bout your crime. ___

With a lit - tle
I ___ said, ___
Then I stood ___

46

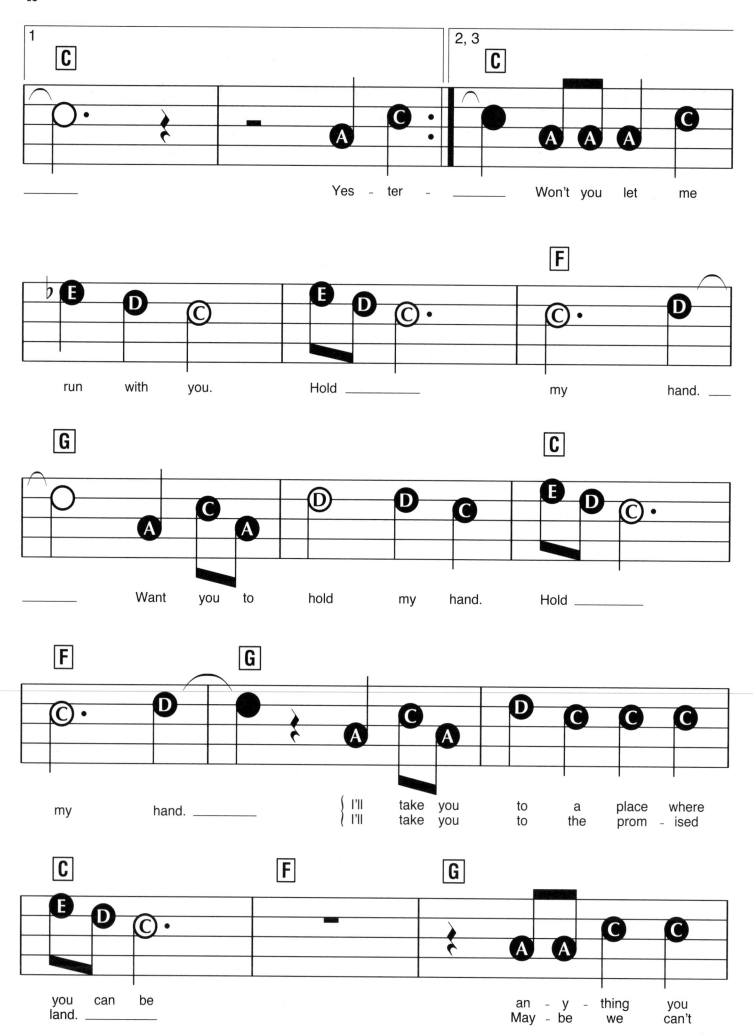

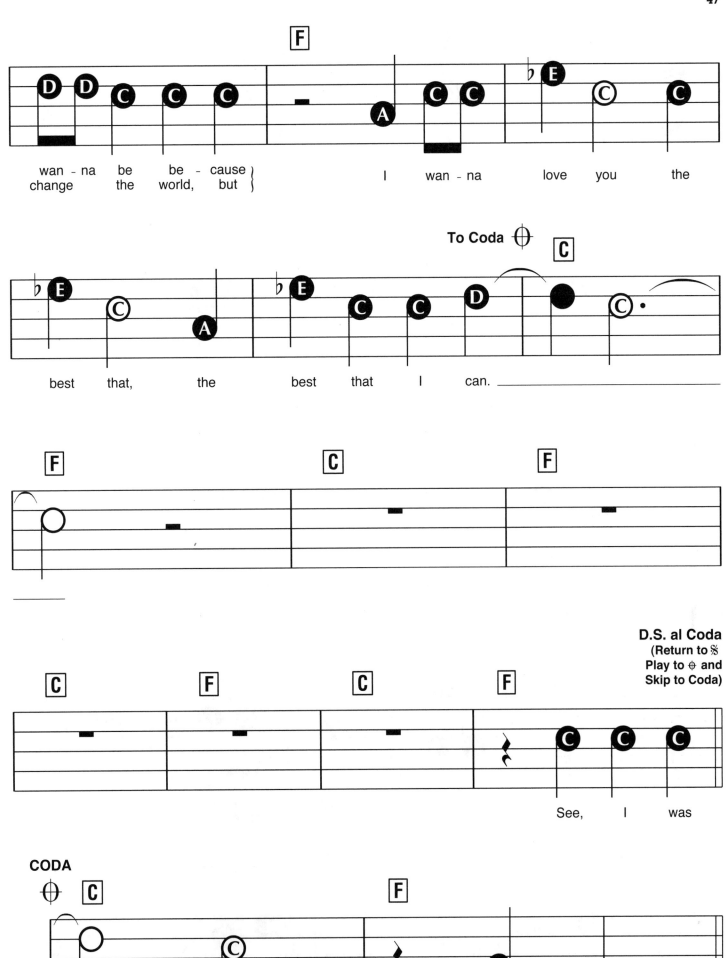

wan - na be be - cause
change the world, but

I wan - na love you the

best that, the
best that I can.

See, I was

Yeah.

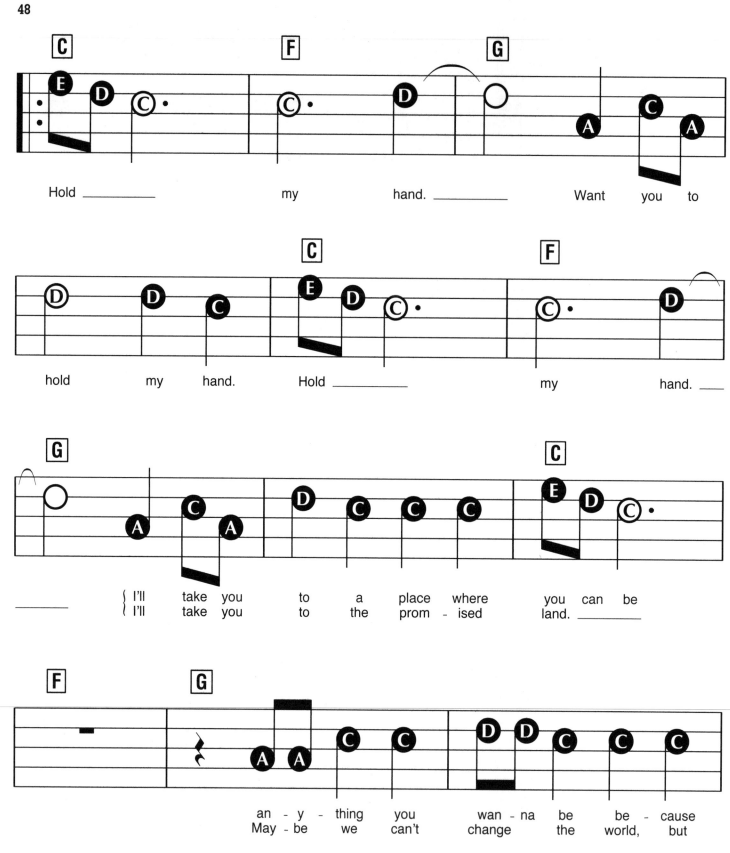

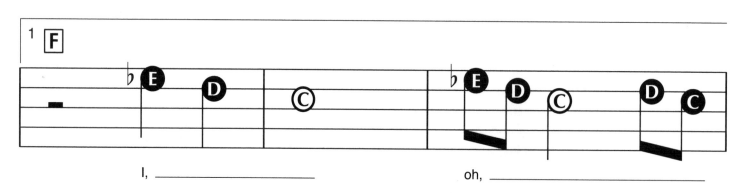

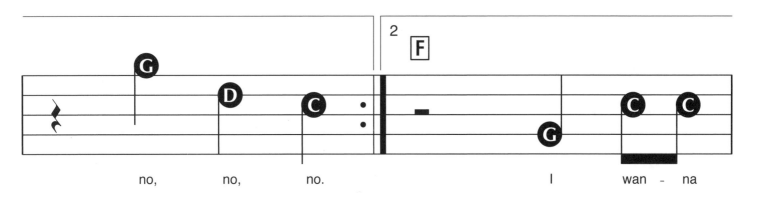

no,   no,   no.   I   wan - na

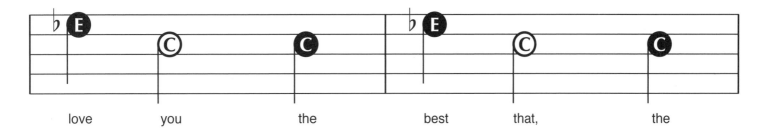

love   you   the   best   that,   the

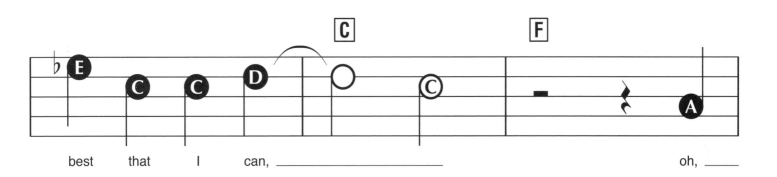

best   that   I   can, _____   oh, _____

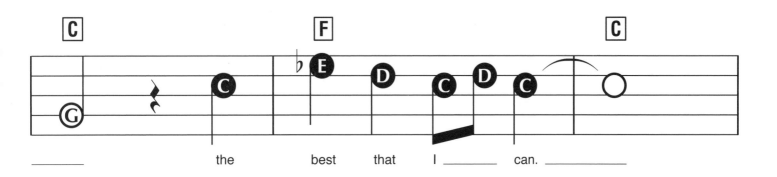

_____   the   best   that   I _____ can. _____

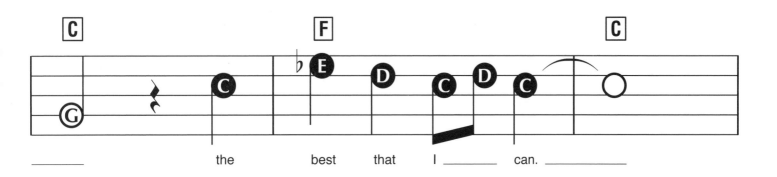

I Fought the Law

Registration 4
Rhythm: Rock

Words and Music by
Sonny Curtis

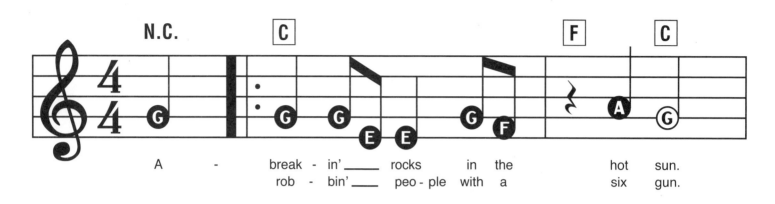

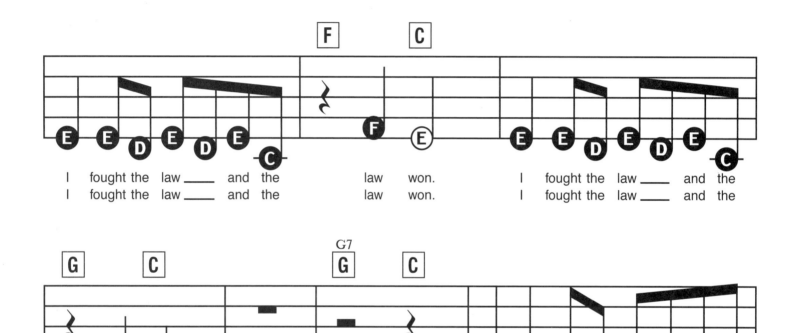

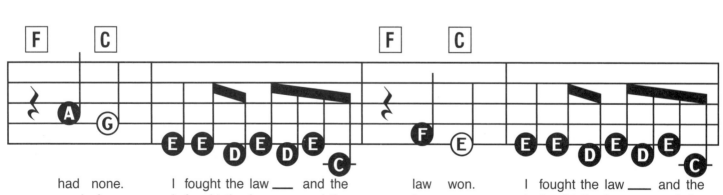

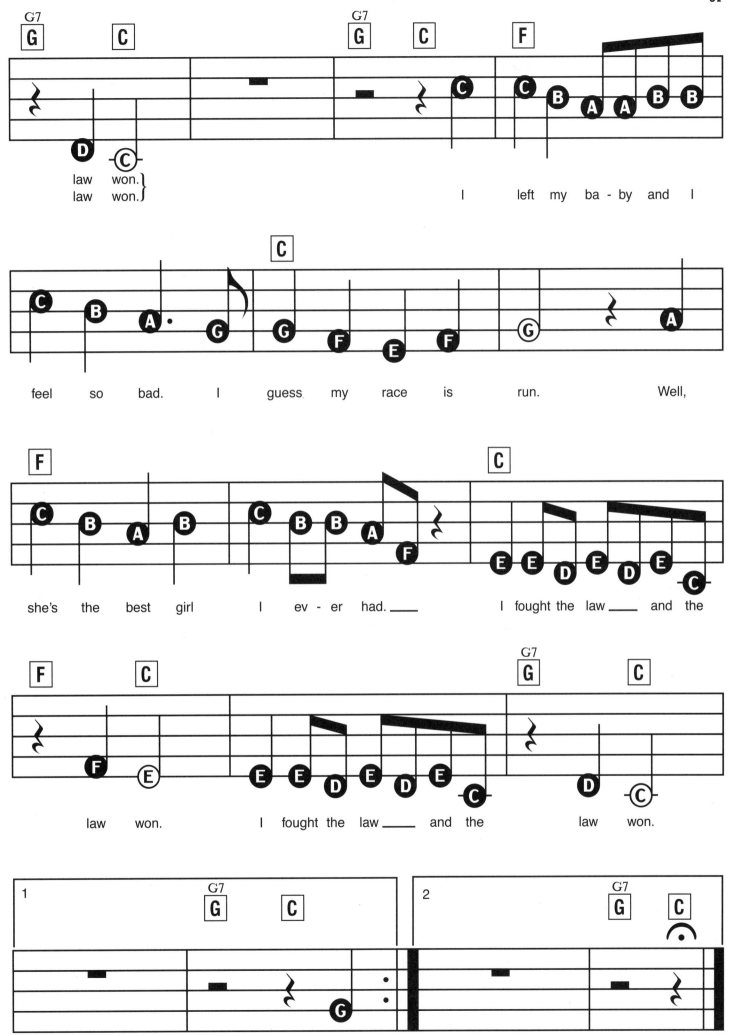

I Still Haven't Found What I'm Looking For

Registration 3
Rhythm: Rock or Disco

Words and Music by
U2

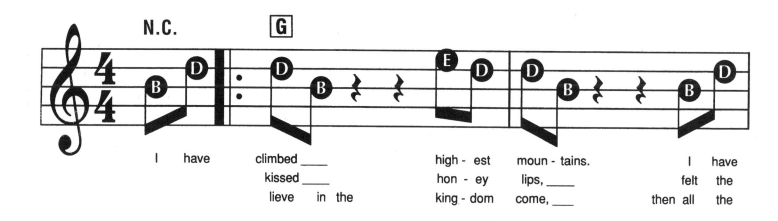

I have climbed ____ high-est moun-tains. I have
kissed ____ hon-ey lips, ____ felt the
lieve in the king-dom come, ___ then all the

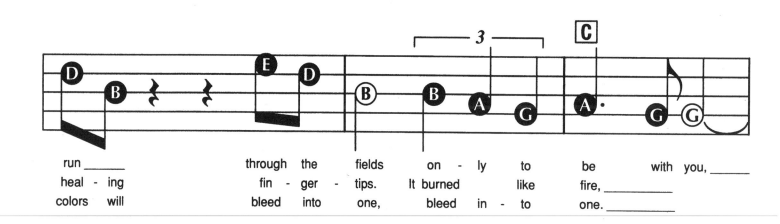

run _____ through the fields on-ly to be with you, _____
heal-ing fin-ger-tips. It burned like fire, _____
colors will bleed into one, bleed in-to one. _____

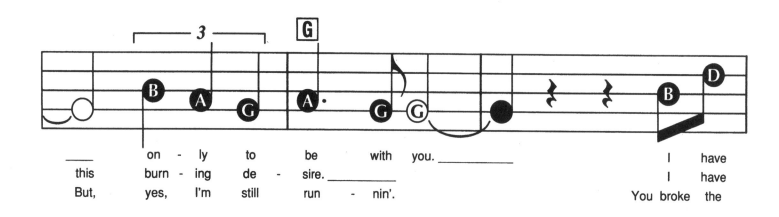

____ on-ly to be with you. _____ I have
this burn-ing de-sire. _____ I have
But, yes, I'm still run-nin'. You broke the

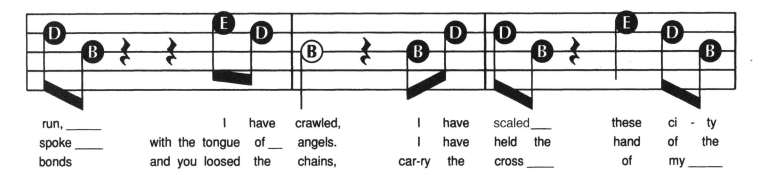

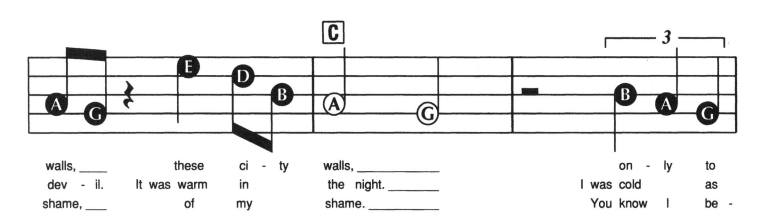

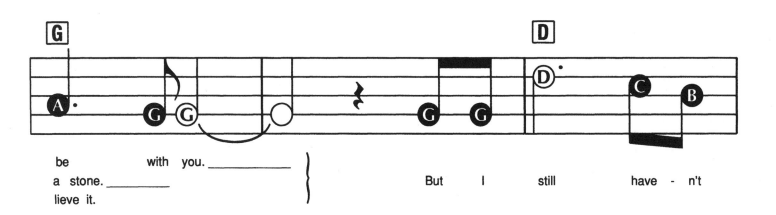

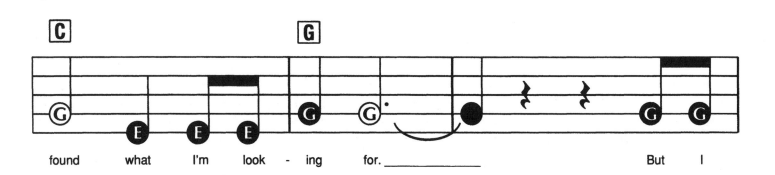

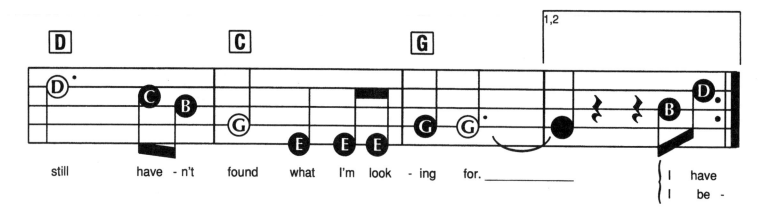

still   have - n't   found   what   I'm   look - ing   for. _____ I have
I be -

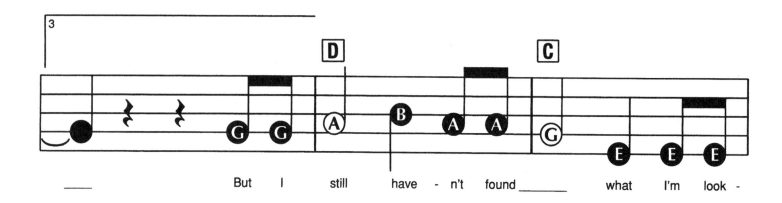

____ But   I   still   have - n't   found _____ what   I'm   look -

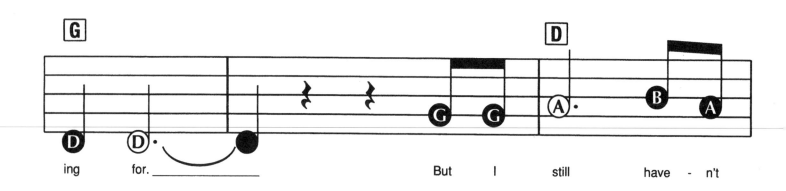

ing   for. _____ But   I   still   have - n't

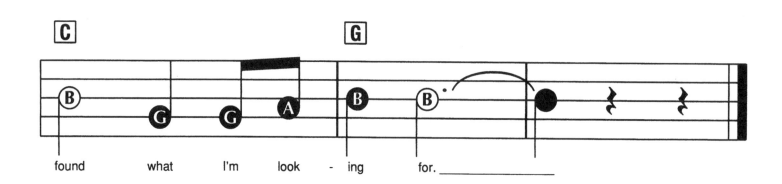

found   what   I'm   look - ing   for. _____

The Joker

Registration 7
Rhythm: Swing, Slow Rock

Words and Music by Steve Miller,
Eddie Curtis and Ahmet Ertegun

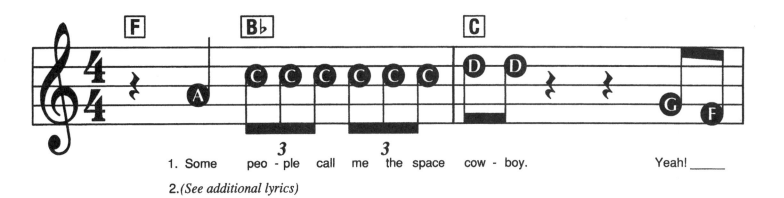

1. Some peo-ple call me the space cow-boy.   Yeah! _____
2. *(See additional lyrics)*

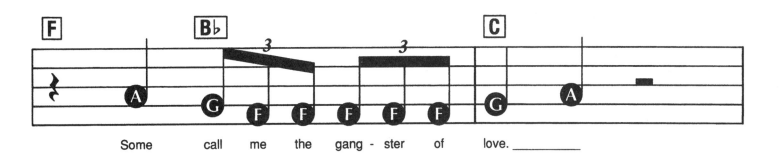

Some call me the gang-ster of love. _____

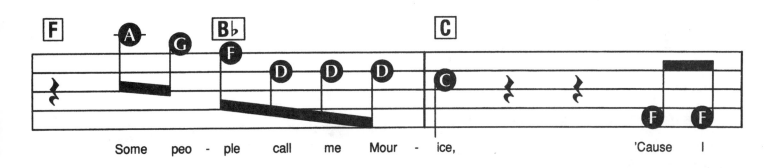

Some peo-ple call me Mour-ice,   'Cause I

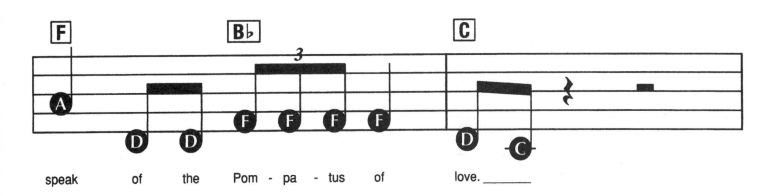

speak of the Pom-pa-tus of love. _____

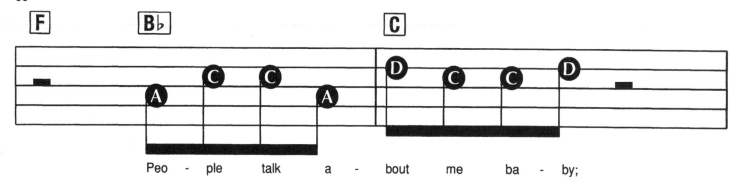

Peo - ple talk a - bout me ba - by;

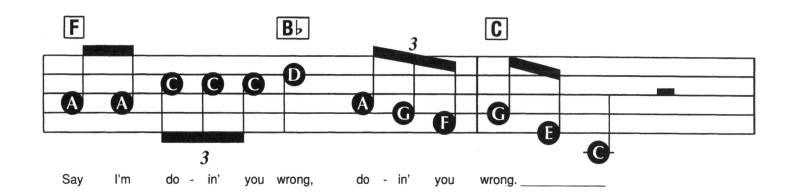

Say I'm do - in' you wrong, do - in' you wrong.

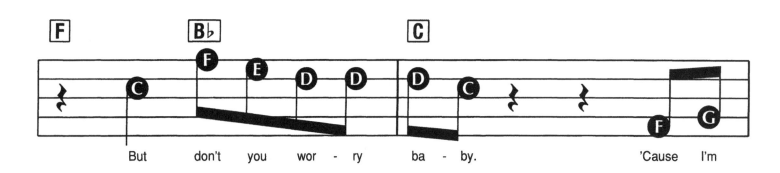

But don't you wor - ry ba - by. 'Cause I'm

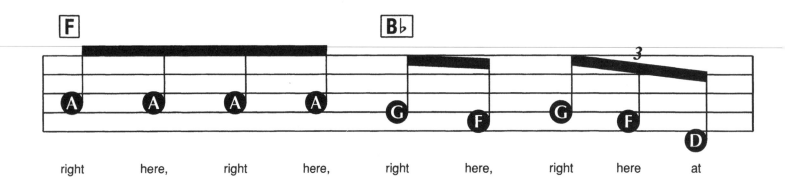

right here, right here, right here, right here at

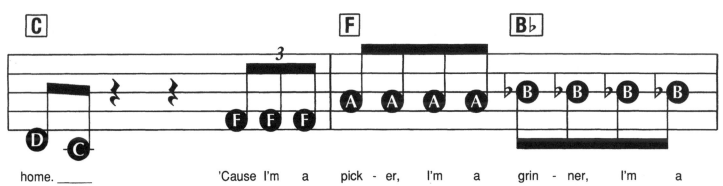

home. 'Cause I'm a pick - er, I'm a grin - ner, I'm a

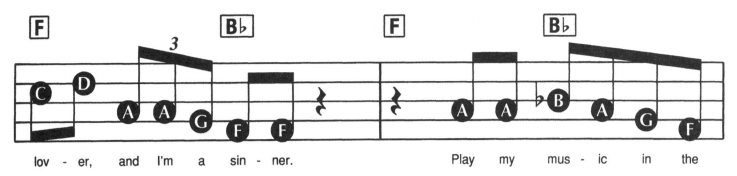

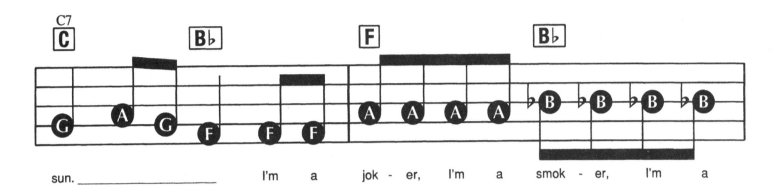

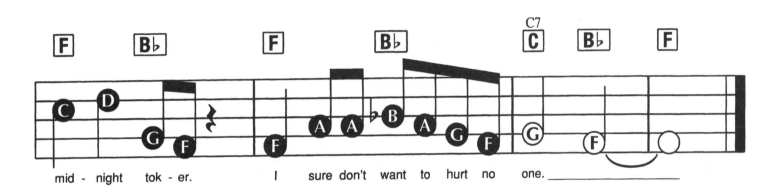

Additional Lyrics

2. You're the cutest thing that I ever did see;
I really love your peaches, want to shake your tree.
Lovey dovey, lovey dovey, lovey dovey all the time;
Come on baby I'll show you a real good time.

Just My Imagination
(Running Away with Me)

Registration 3
Rhythm: Rock or 8-Beat

Words and Music by Norman Whitfield
and Barrett Strong

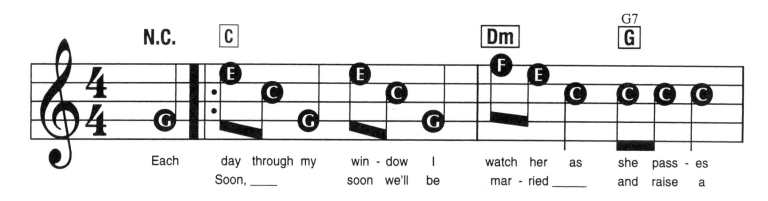

Each day through my win - dow I watch her as she pass - es
Soon, ____ soon we'll be mar - ried ____ and raise a

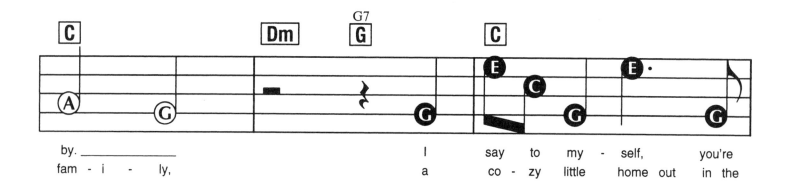

by. _____ I say to my - self, you're
fam - i - ly, a co - zy little home out in the

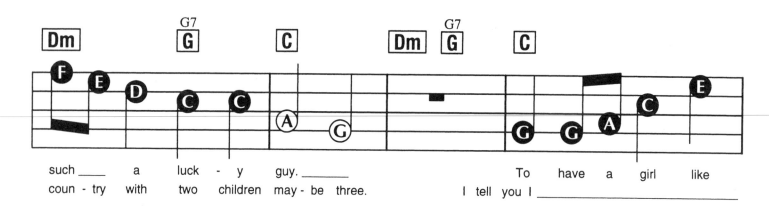

such ____ a luck - y guy. _____ To have a girl like
coun - try with two children may - be three. I tell you I _____

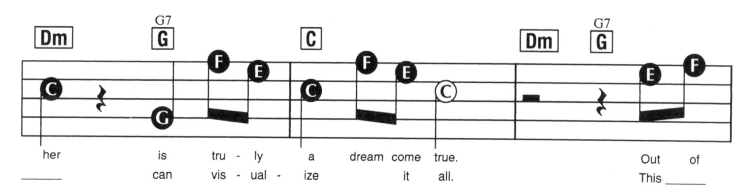

her is tru - ly a dream come true. Out of
can vis - ual - ize it all. This ____

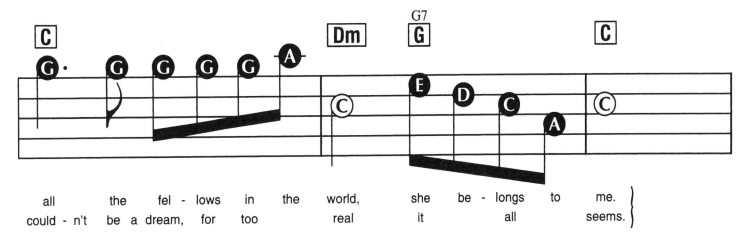

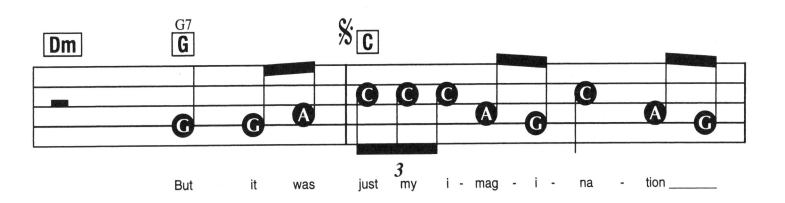

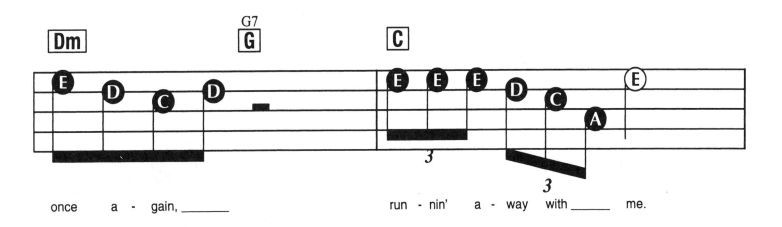

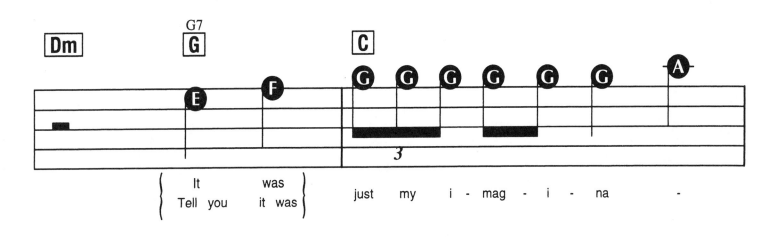

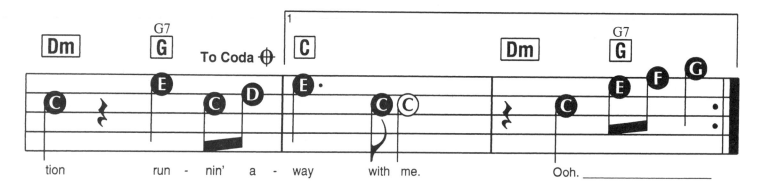

tion run - nin' a - way with me. Ooh. _____

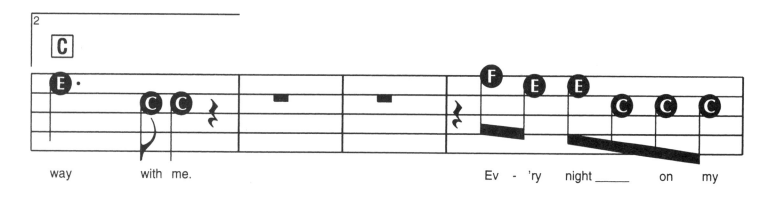

way with me. Ev - 'ry night _____ on my

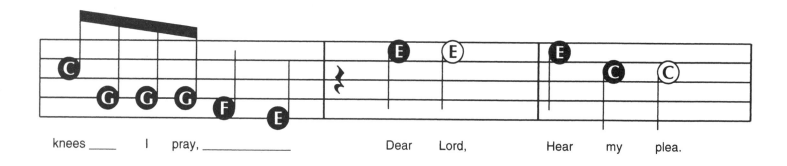

knees _____ I pray, _____ Dear Lord, Hear my plea.

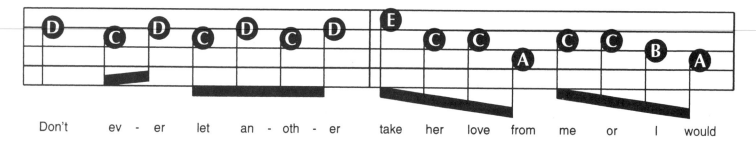

Don't ev - er let an - oth - er take her love from me or I would

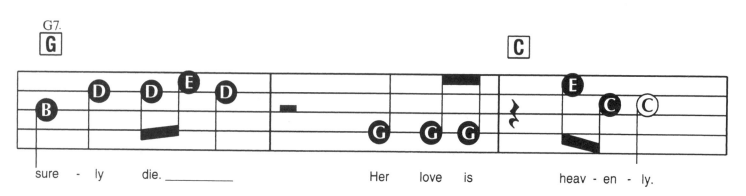

sure - ly die. _____ Her love is heav - en - ly.

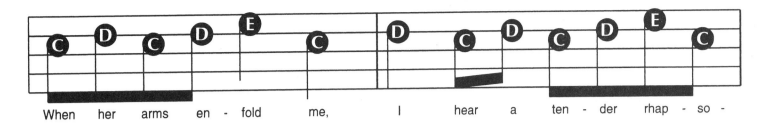

When her arms en - fold me, I hear a ten - der rhap - so -

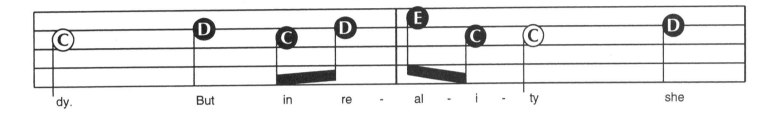

dy. But in re - al - i - ty she

D.S. al Coda
(Return to %
Play to ⊕ and
Skip to Coda)

CODA

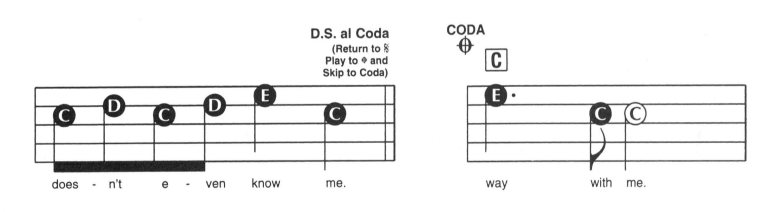

does - n't e - ven know me.

way with me.

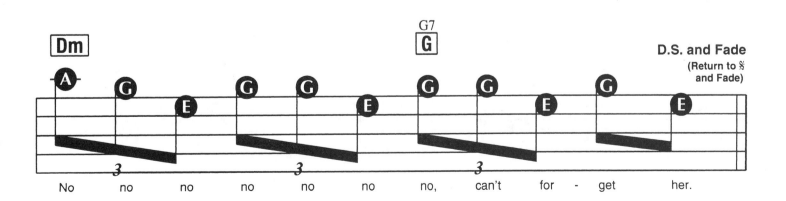

No no no no no no no, can't for - get her.

Kansas City

Registration 4
Rhythm: Shuffle or Swing

Words and Music by Jerry Leiber
and Mike Stoller

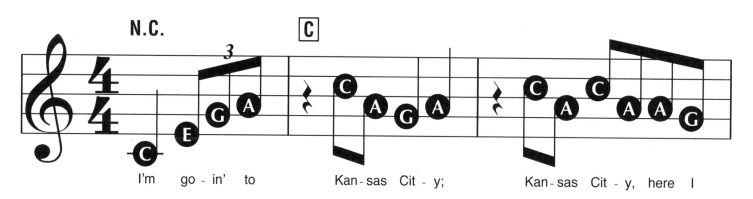

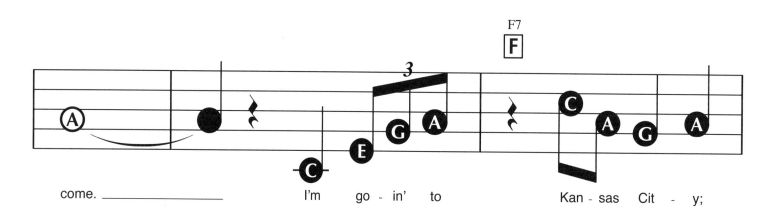

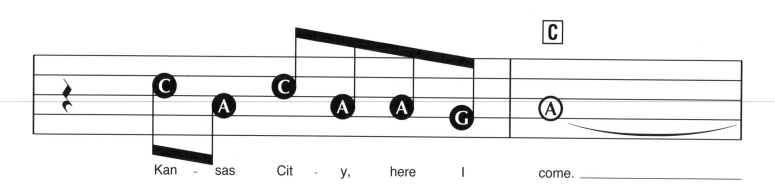

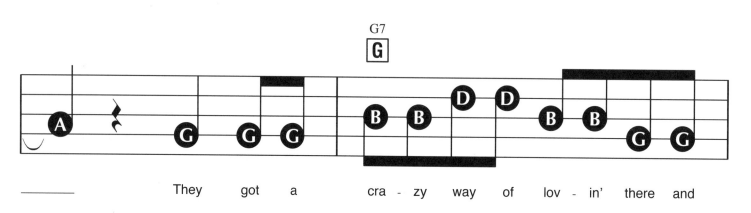

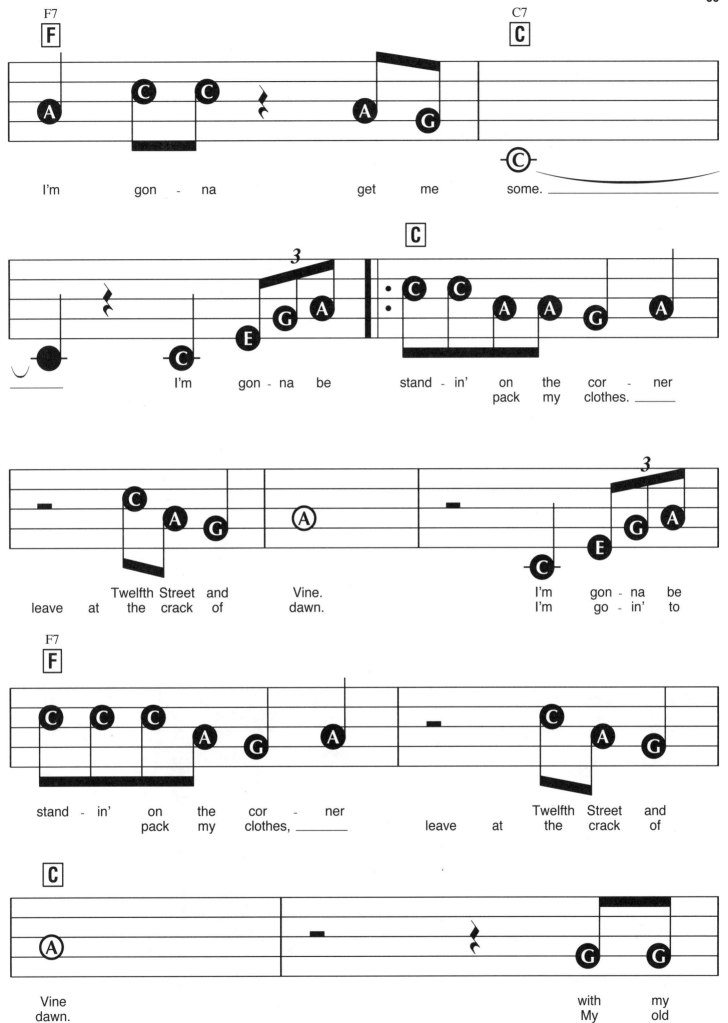

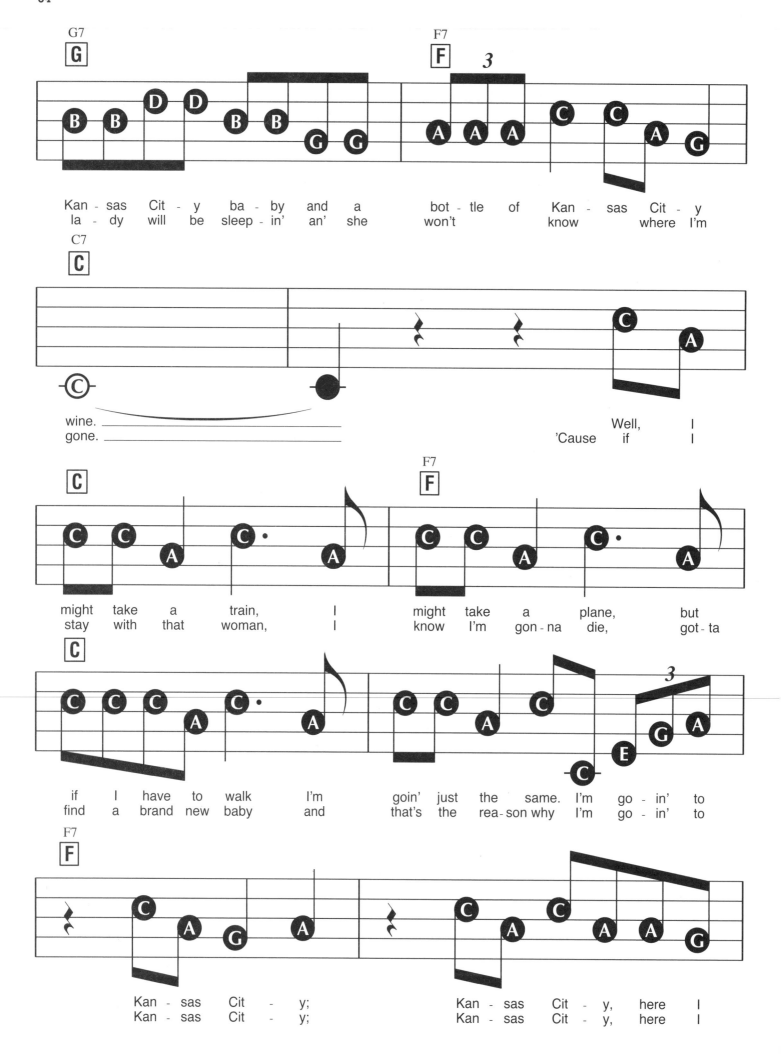

65

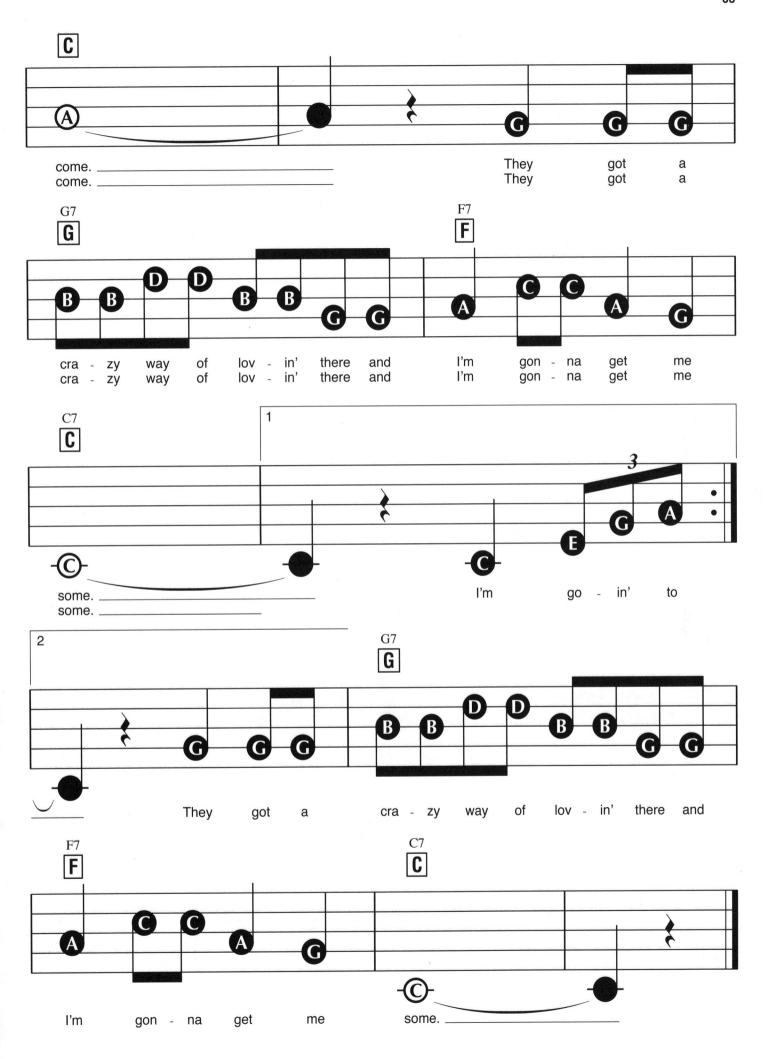

Kiss

Registration 4
Rhythm: Funk or Rock

Words and Music by
Prince

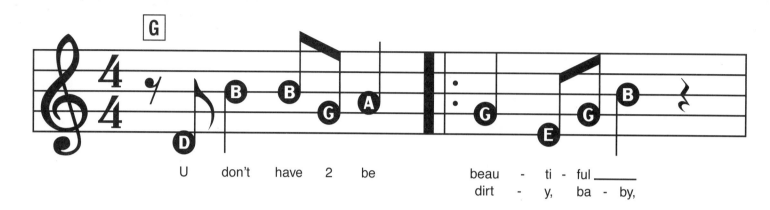

U don't have 2 be beau - ti - ful _____
dirt - y, ba - by,

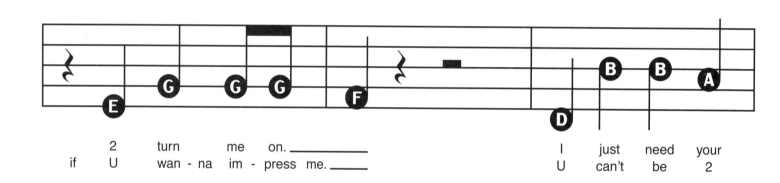

2 turn me on. _____ I just need your
if U wan - na im - press me. _____ U can't be 2

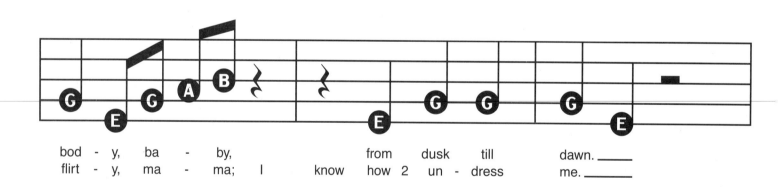

bod - y, ba - by, from dusk till dawn. _____
flirt - y, ma - ma; I know how 2 un - dress me. _____

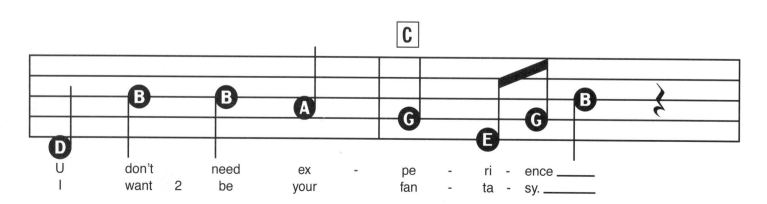

U don't need ex - pe - ri - ence _____
I want 2 be your fan - ta - sy. _____

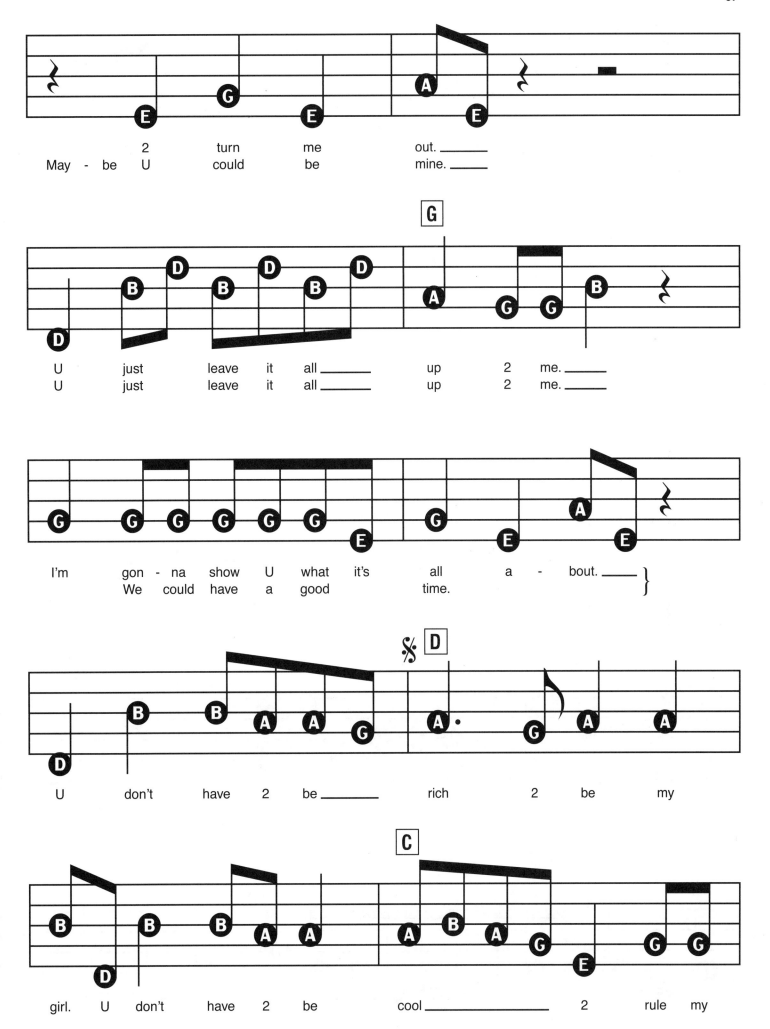

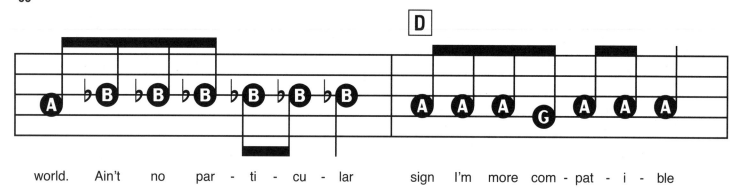

world. Ain't no par - ti - cu - lar   sign I'm more com - pat - i - ble

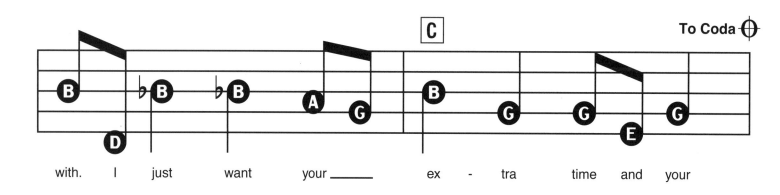

To Coda ⊕

with. I just want your _____ ex - tra time and your

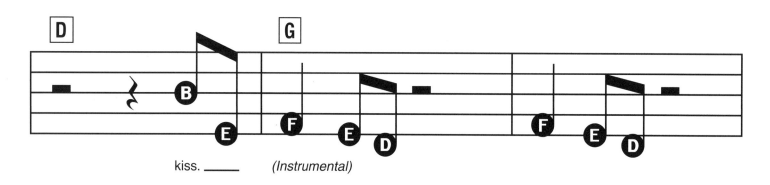

kiss. _____ *(Instrumental)*

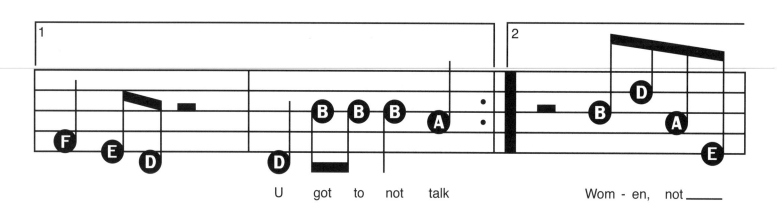

U got to not talk   Wom - en, not _____

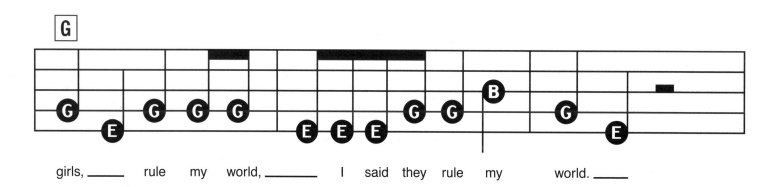

girls, _____ rule my world, _____ I said they rule my world. _____

69

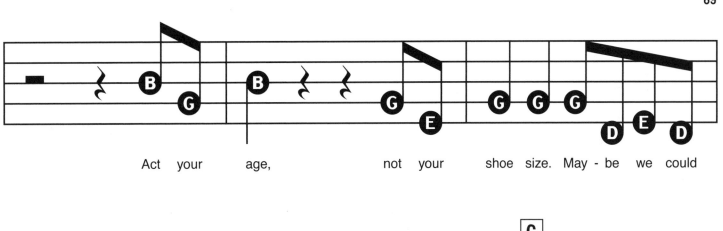

Act your age, not your shoe size. May - be we could

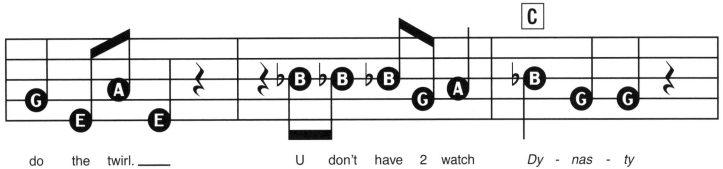

do the twirl. _____ U don't have 2 watch *Dy - nas - ty*

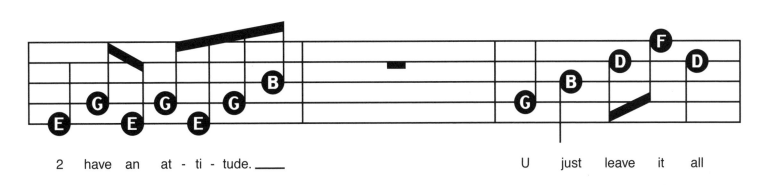

2 have an at - ti - tude. _____ U just leave it all

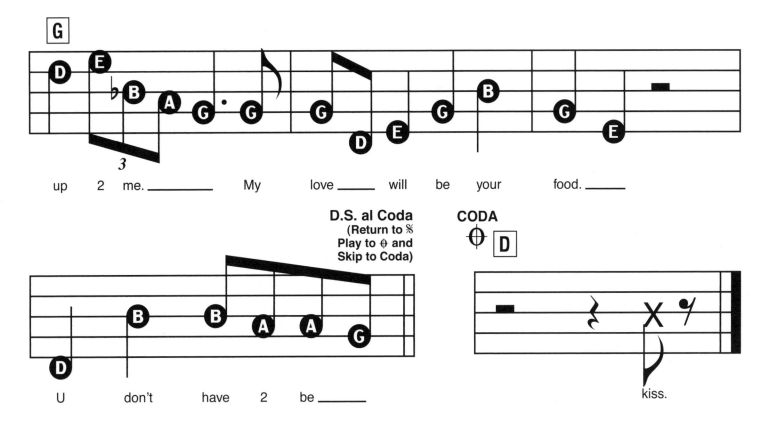

up 2 me. _____ My love _____ will be your food. _____

D.S. al Coda
(Return to %
Play to ⊕ and
Skip to Coda)

CODA

U don't have 2 be _____

kiss.

La Bamba

Registration 4
Rhythm: Latin

By Richard Valenzuela

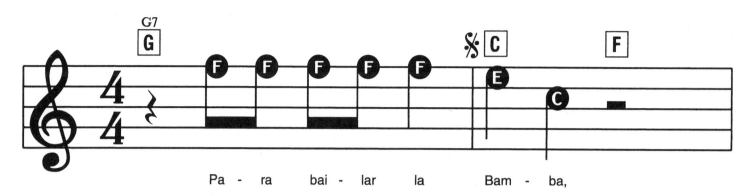

Pa - ra bai - lar la Bam - ba,

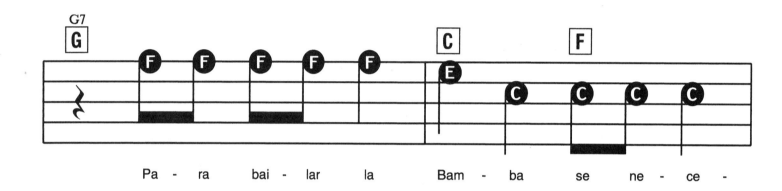

Pa - ra bai - lar la Bam - ba se ne - ce -

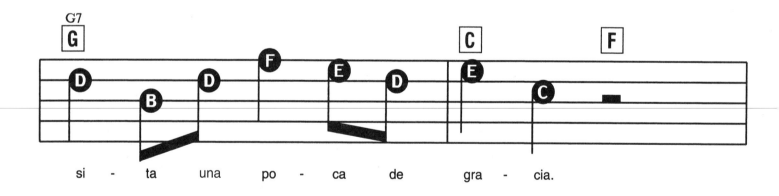

si - ta una po - ca de gra - cia.

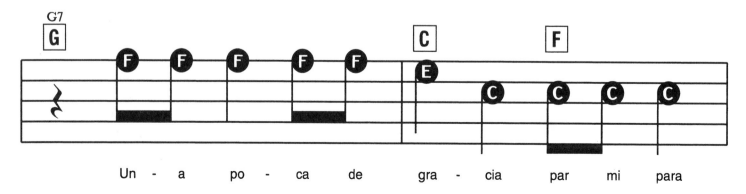

Un - a po - ca de gra - cia par mi para

71

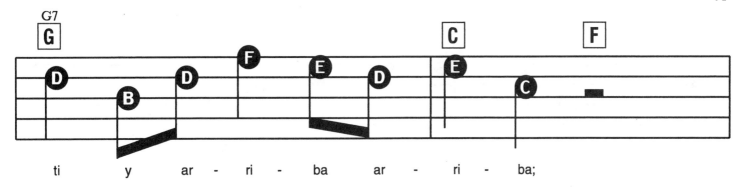

ti y ar - ri - ba ar - ri - ba;

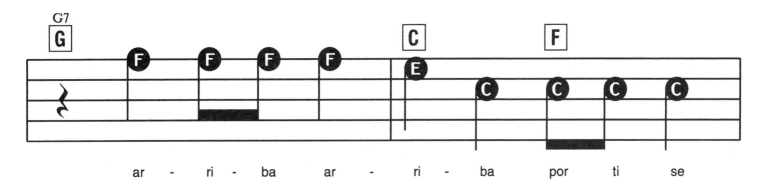

ar - ri - ba ar - ri - ba por ti se

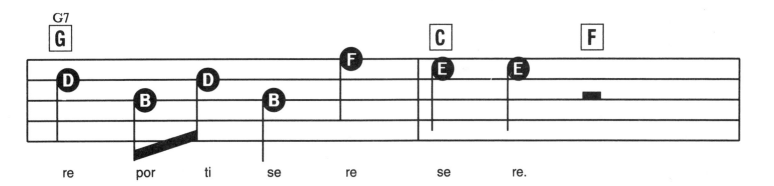

re por ti se re se re.

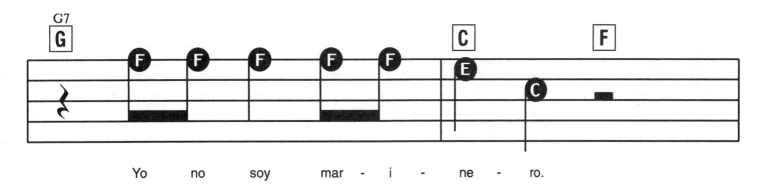

Yo no soy mar - i - ne - ro.

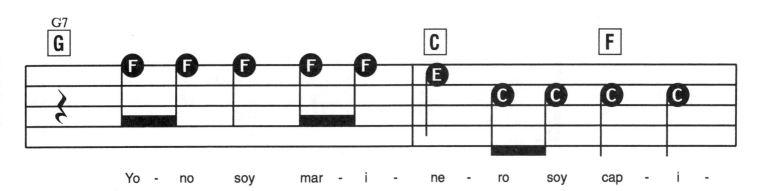

Yo - no soy mar - i - ne - ro soy cap - i -

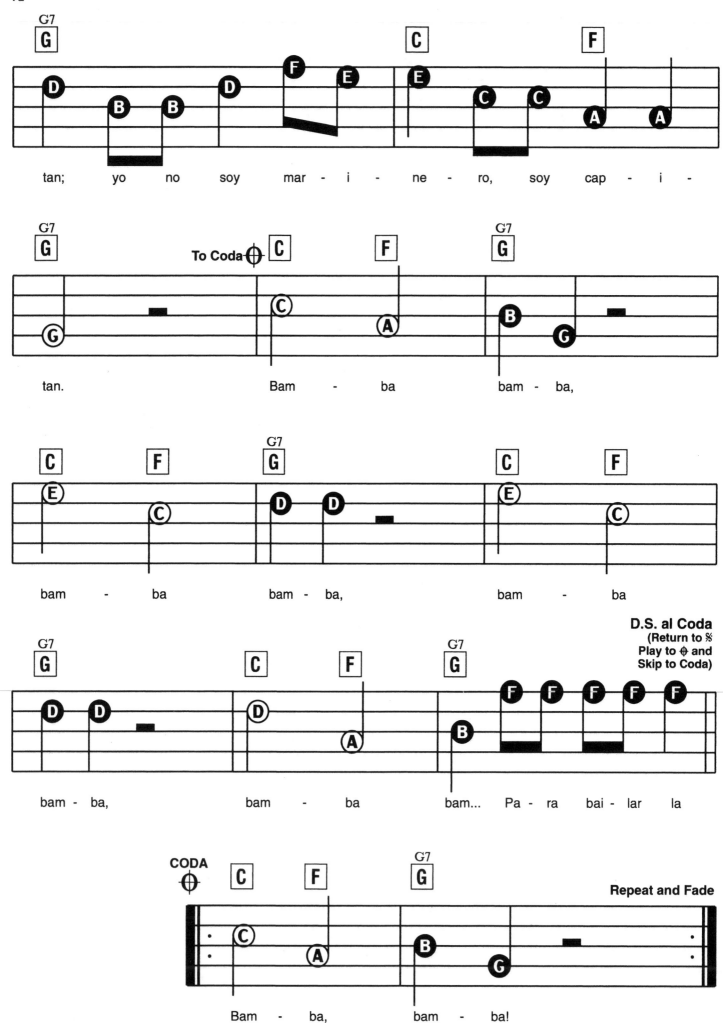

Lean on Me

Registration 8
Rhythm: Rock or 8-Beat

Words and Music by
Bill Withers

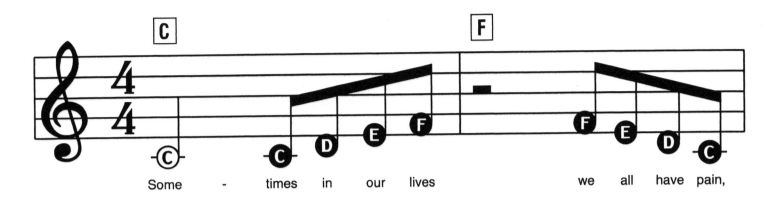

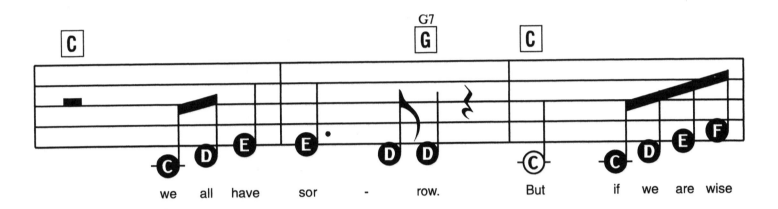

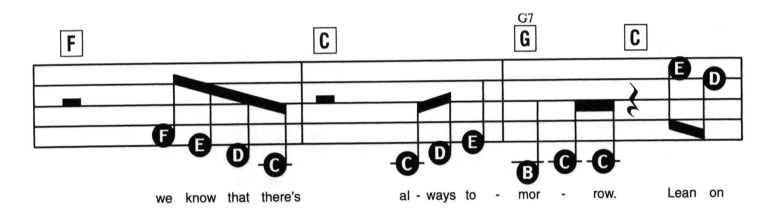

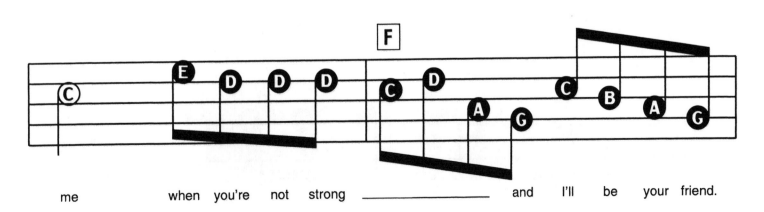

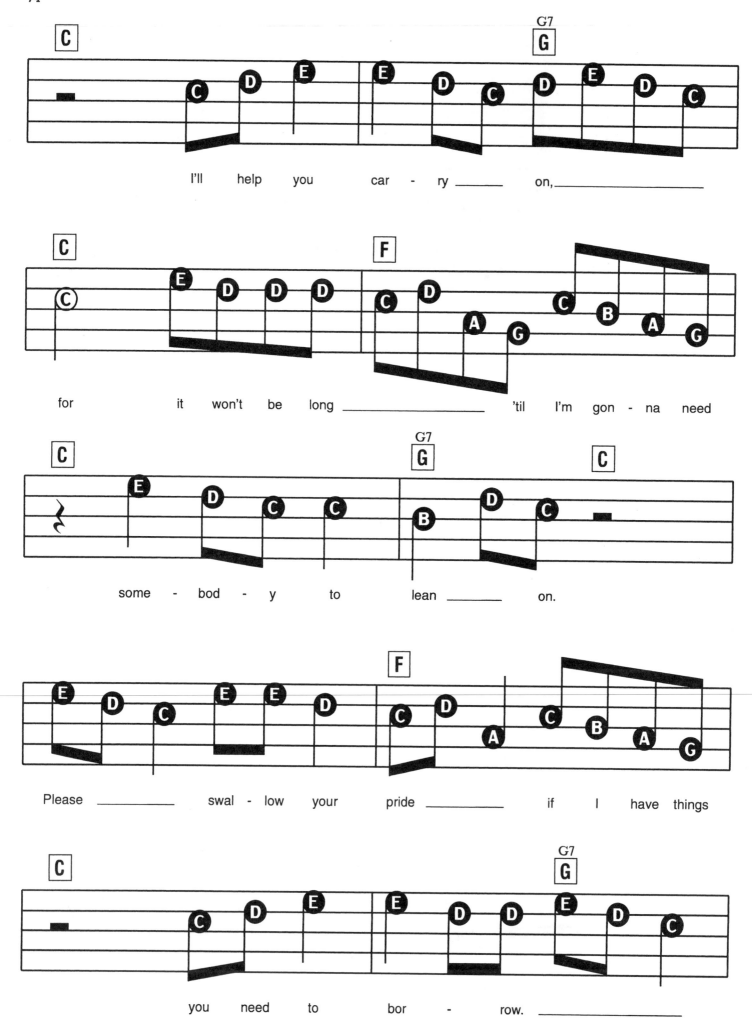

75

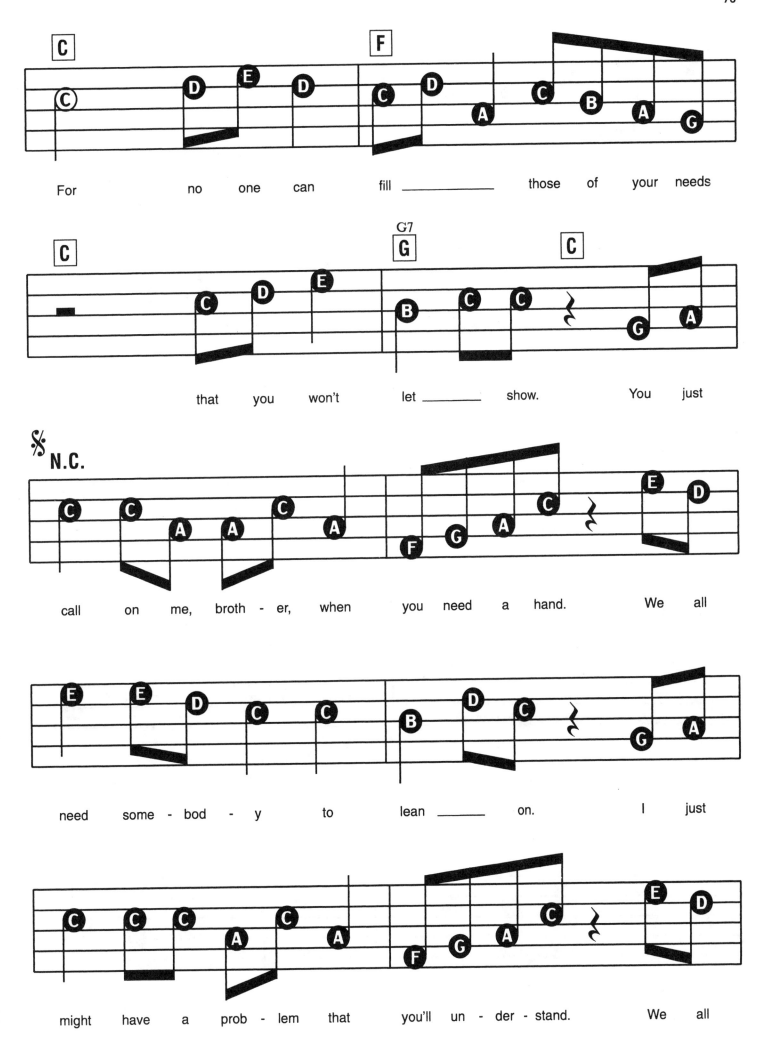

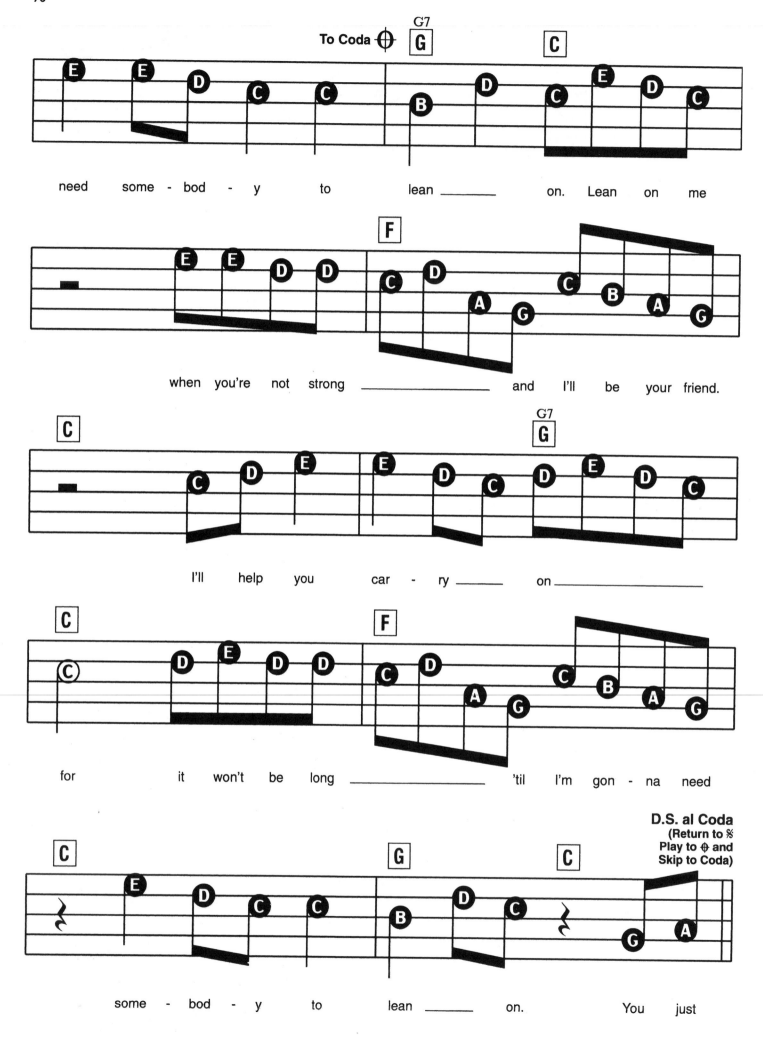

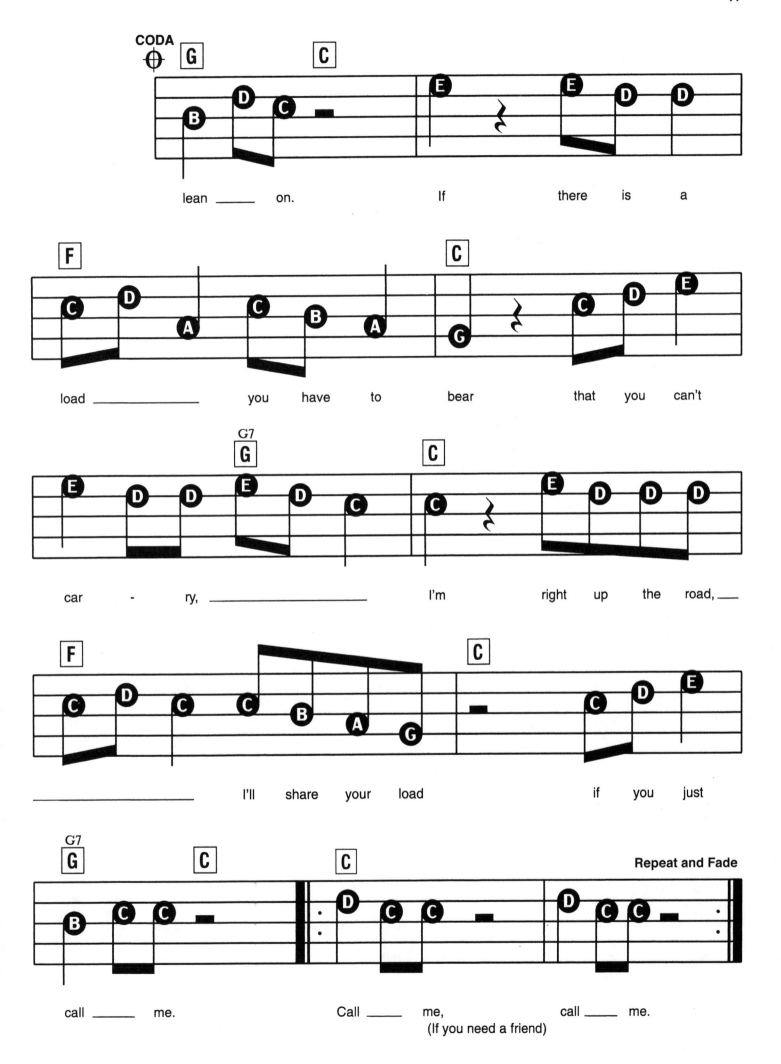

Lay Down Sally

Registration 9
Rhythm: Rock or 8-Beat

Words and Music by Eric Clapton,
Marcy Levy and George Terry

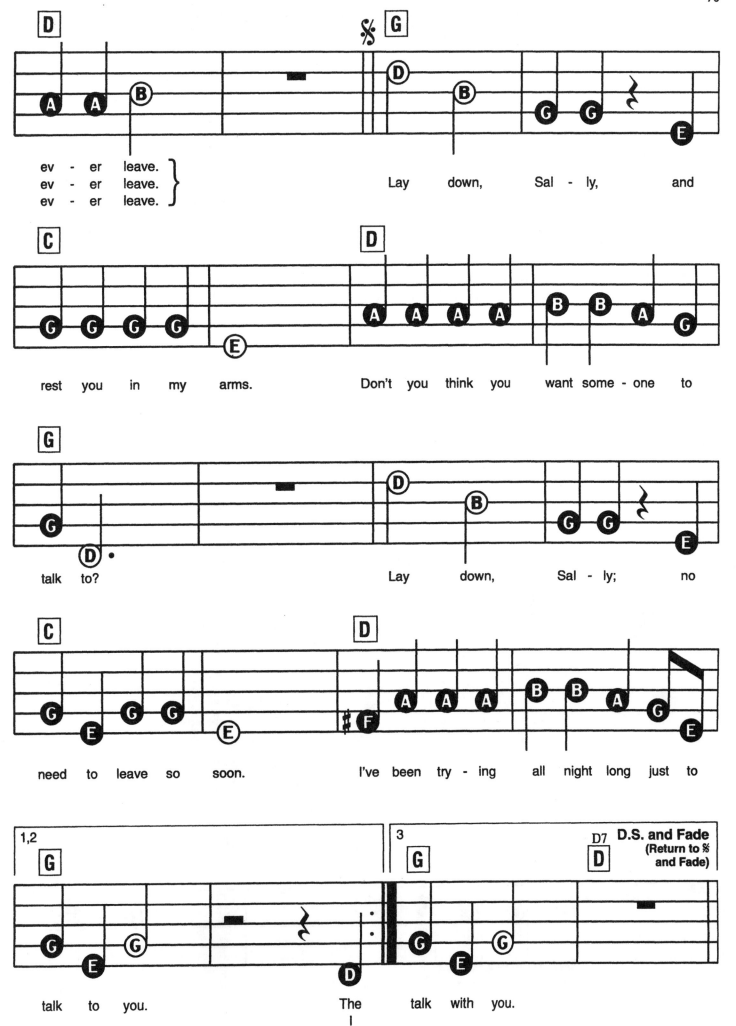

Leaving on a Jet Plane

Registration 1
Rhythm: Rock or Slow Rock

Words and Music by
John Denver

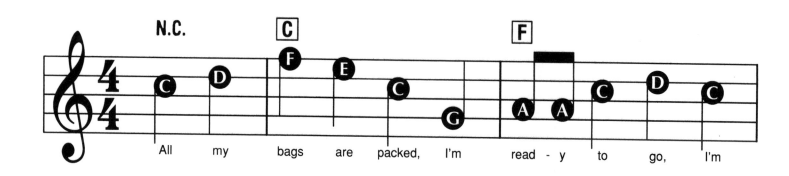

All my bags are packed, I'm read - y to go, I'm

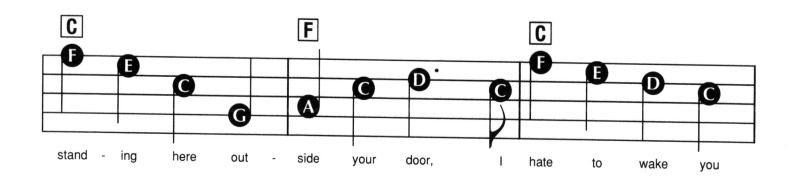

stand - ing here out - side your door, I hate to wake you

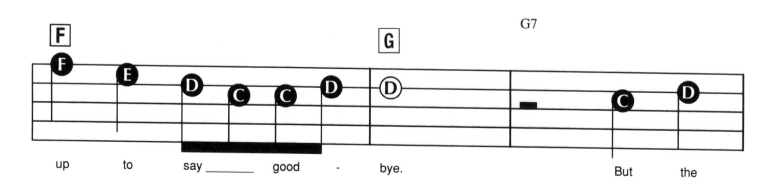

up to say _____ good - bye. But the

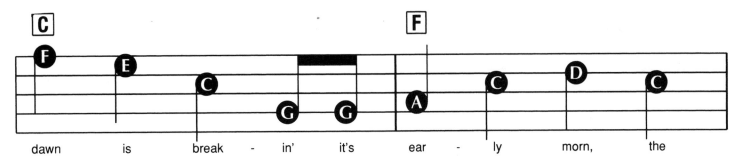

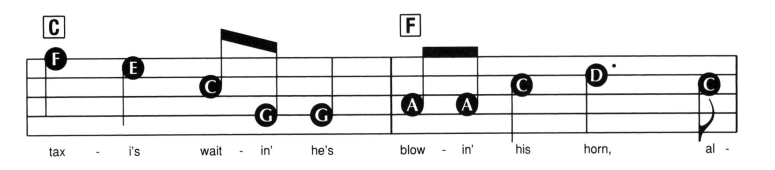

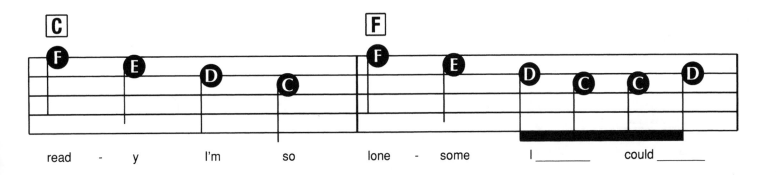

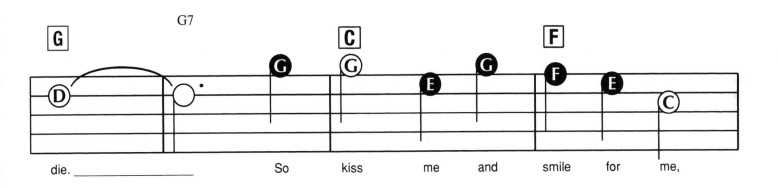

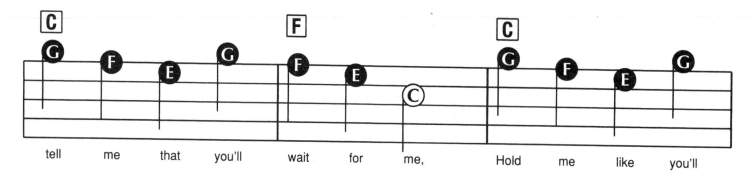

tell   me   that   you'll   wait   for   me,   Hold   me   like   you'll

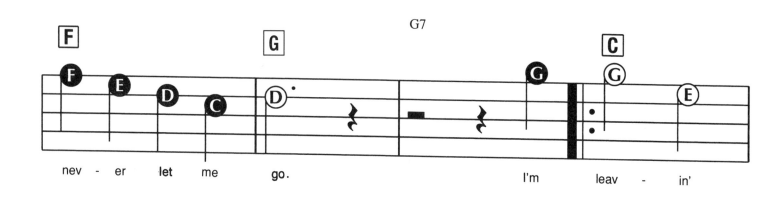

nev - er   let   me   go.   I'm   leav - in'

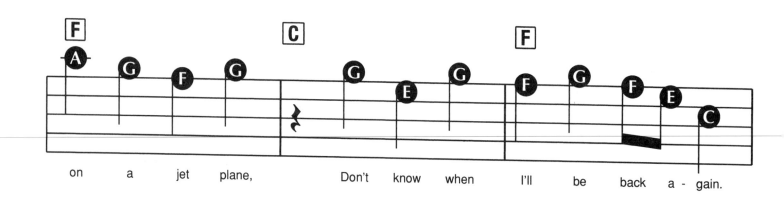

on   a   jet   plane,   Don't   know   when   I'll   be   back   a - gain.

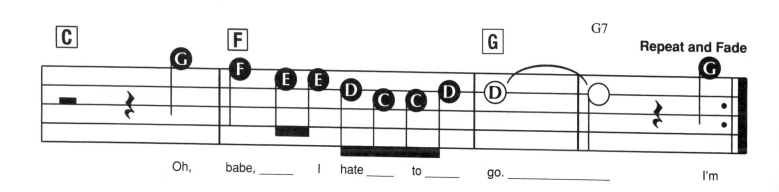

Oh,   babe, _____   I   hate _____   to _____   go. _____   I'm

Riptide

Registration 4
Rhythm: Rock or Dance

Words and Music by
Vance Joy

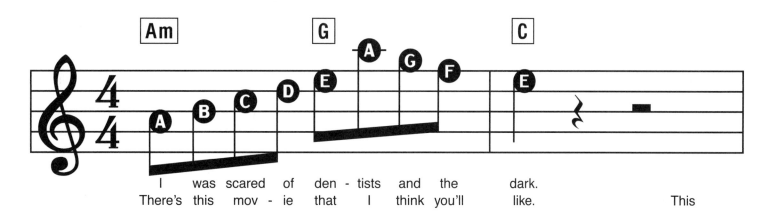

I was scared of den - tists and the dark. This
There's this mov - ie that I think you'll like.

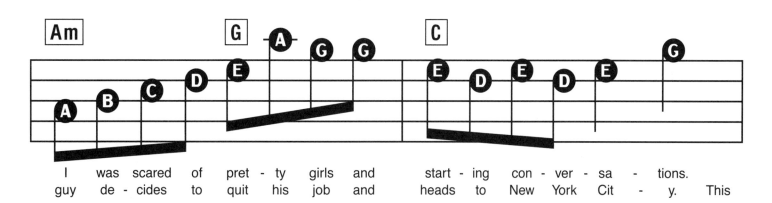

I was scared of pret - ty girls and start - ing con - ver - sa - tions.
guy de - cides to quit his job and heads to New York Cit - y. This

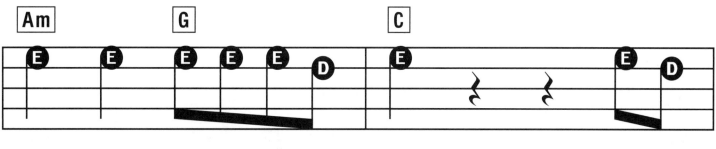

All my friends are turn - ing green; you're the
cow - boy's run - ning from him - self, and

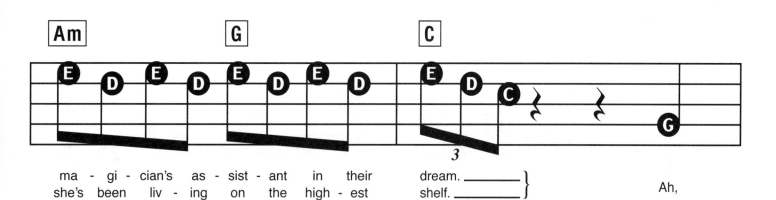

ma - gi - cian's as - sist - ant in their dream. _____ }
she's been liv - ing on the high - est shelf. _____ }

Ah,

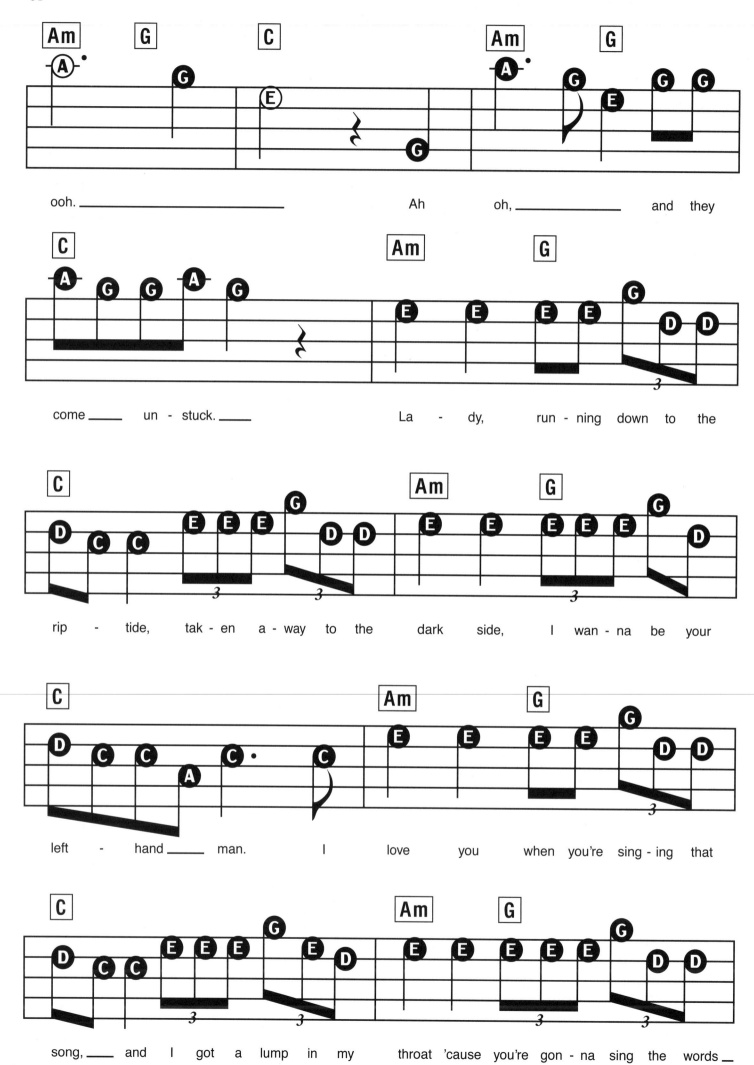

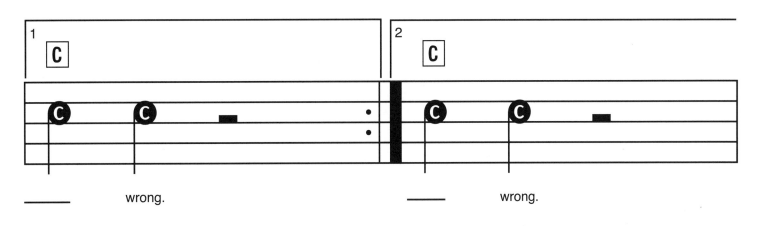

1 **C**

2 **C**

_____ wrong.   _____ wrong.

N.C.

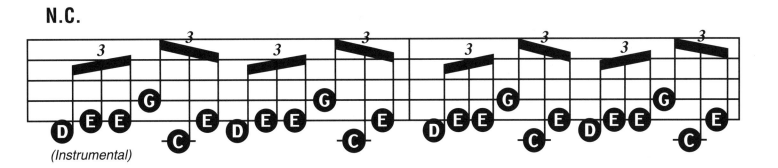

(Instrumental)

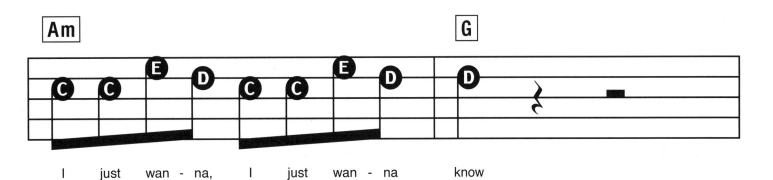

Am   **G**

I just wan - na, I just wan - na know

C   **F**

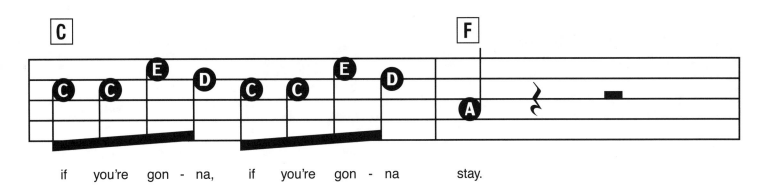

if you're gon - na, if you're gon - na stay.

Am   **G**

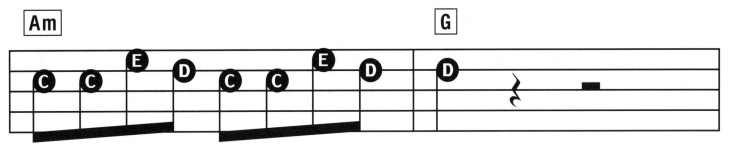

I just got - ta, I just got - ta know;

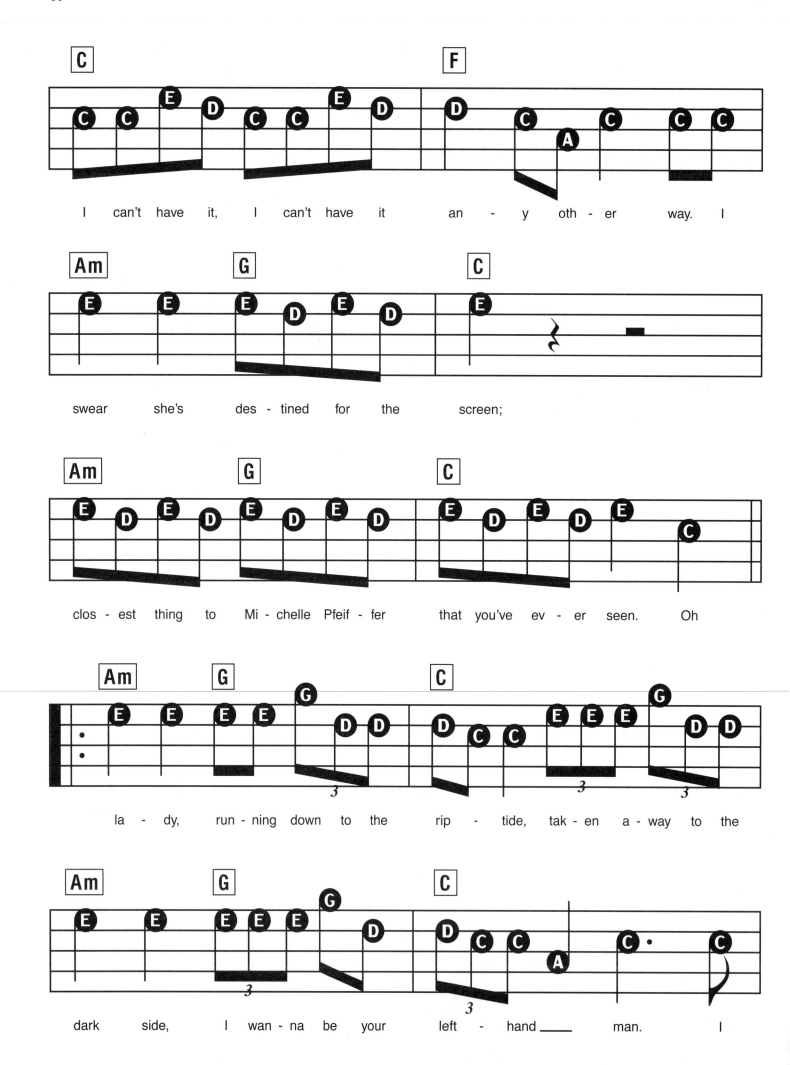

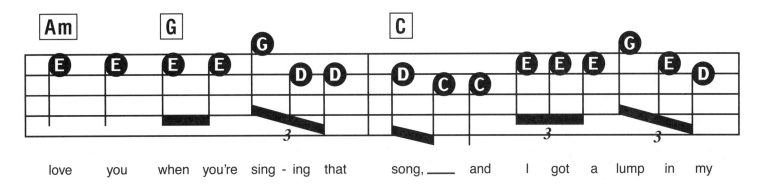

love   you   when you're sing - ing that   song,___ and   I   got a   lump in my

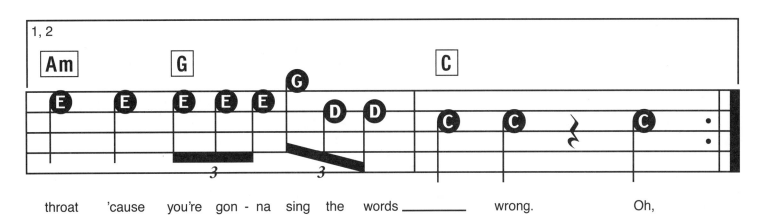

throat   'cause you're gon - na sing the words_____ wrong.   Oh,

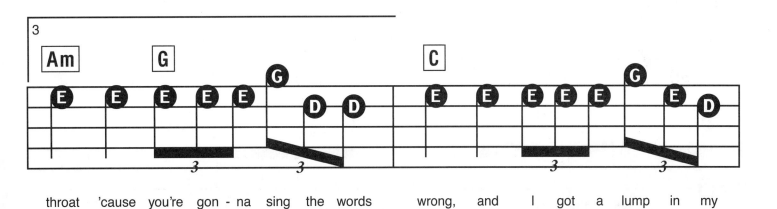

throat   'cause you're gon - na sing the words   wrong, and   I   got a   lump in my

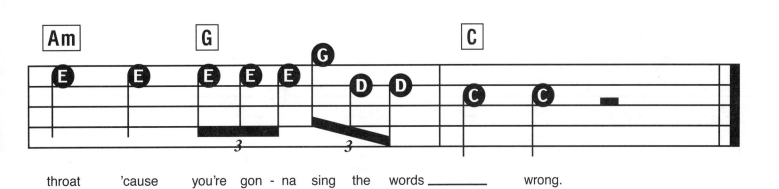

throat   'cause   you're gon - na sing the words_____ wrong.

Louie, Louie

Registration 5
Rhythm: Rock

Words and Music by
Richard Berry

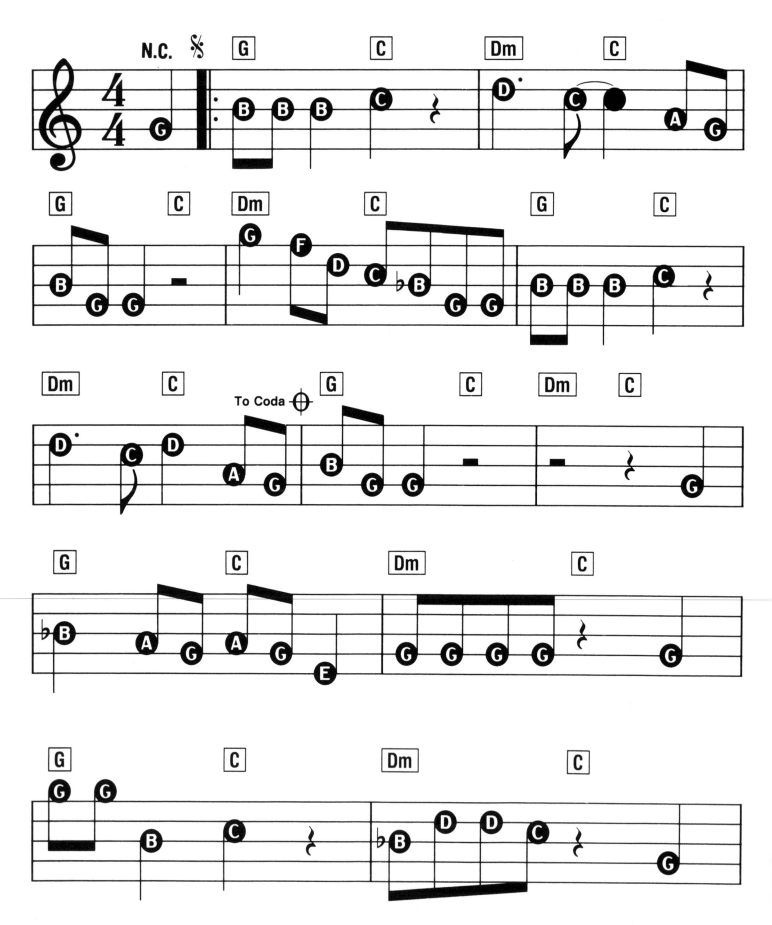

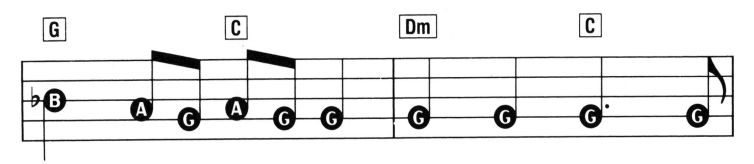

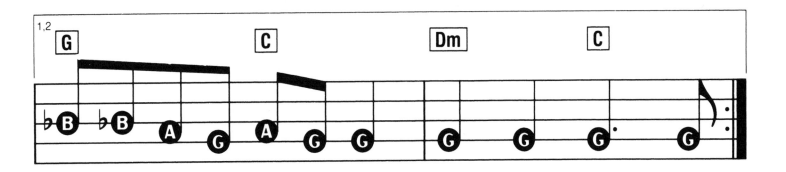

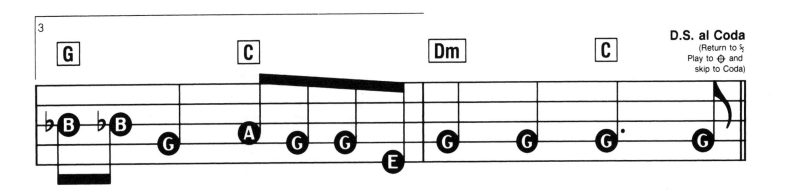

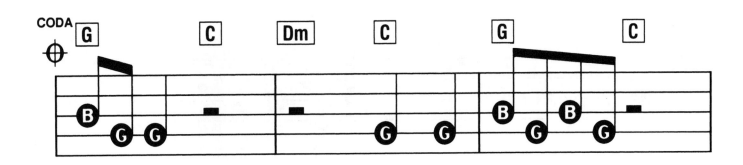

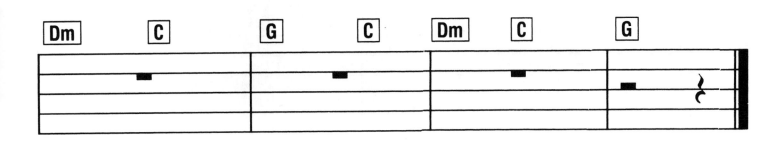

Love Me Do

Registration 4
Rhythm: Rock

Words and Music by John Lennon
and Paul McCartney

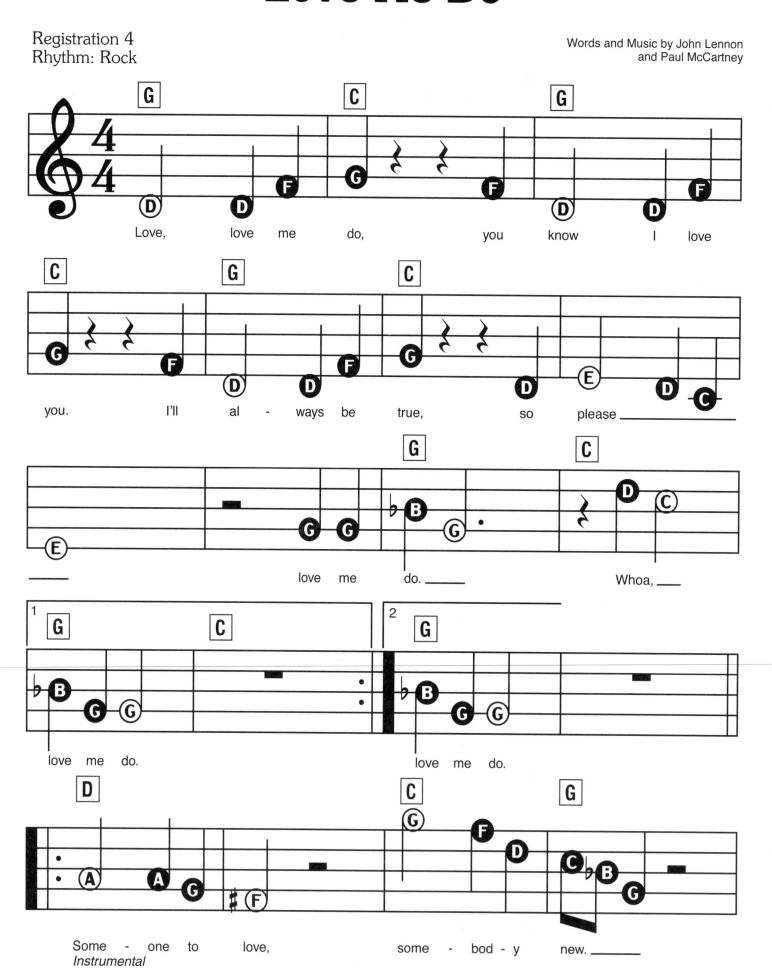

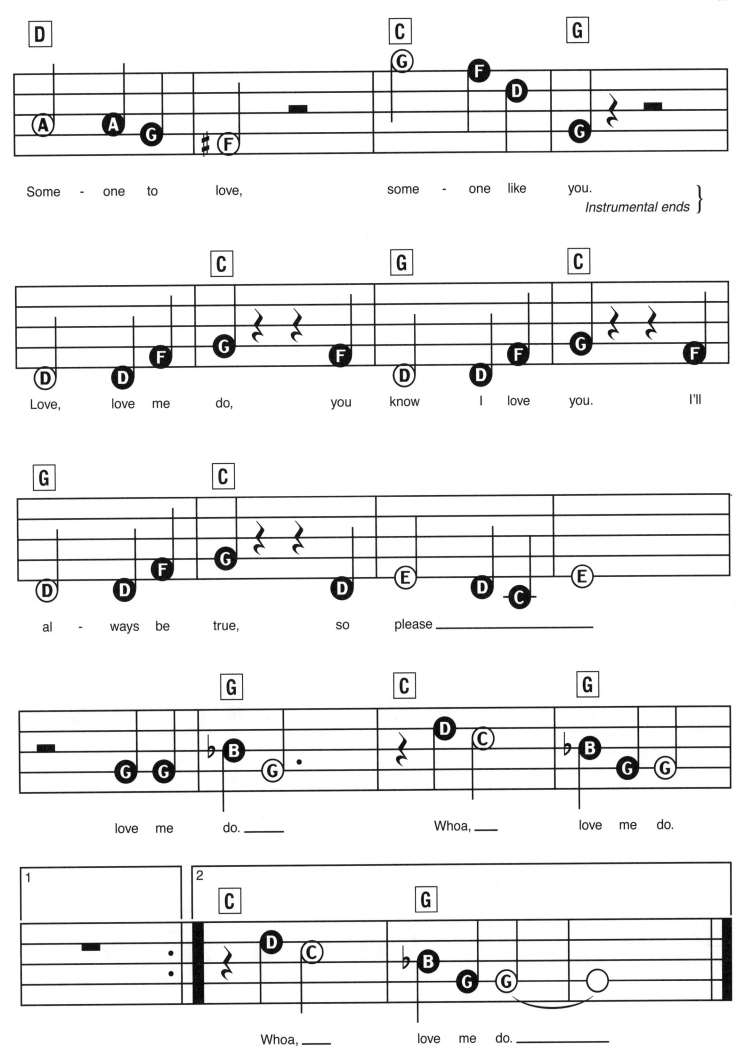

Me and Bobby McGee

Registration 4
Rhythm: Country Rock

Words and Music by Kris Kristofferson
and Fred Foster

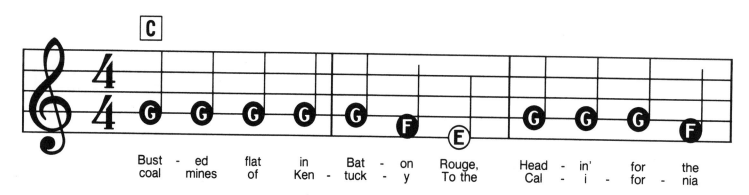

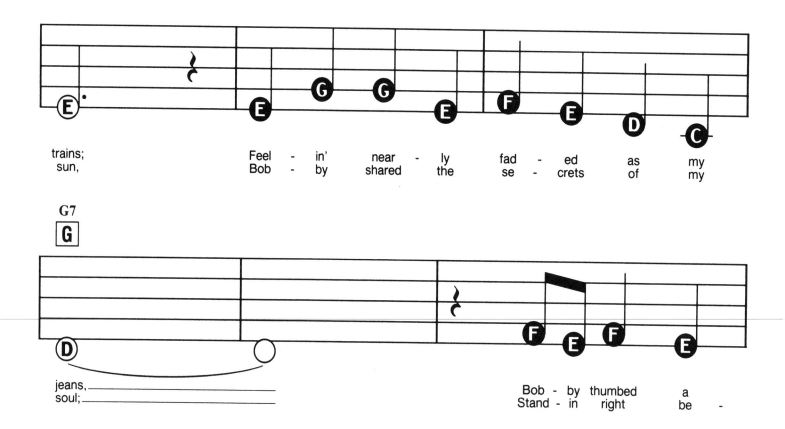

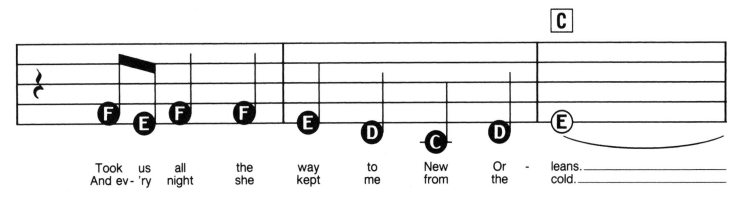

Took us all the way to New Or - leans._____
And ev - 'ry night she kept me from the cold._____

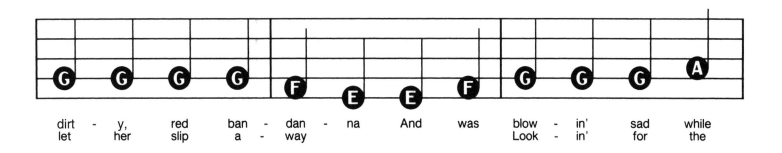

_____ Then I took my har - poon out of my
_____ some - where near Sa - lin - as, Lord I

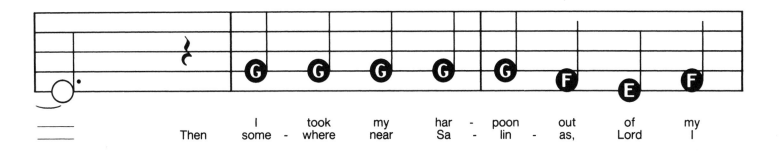

dirt - y, red ban - dan - na And was blow - in' sad while
let her slip a - way Look - in' for the

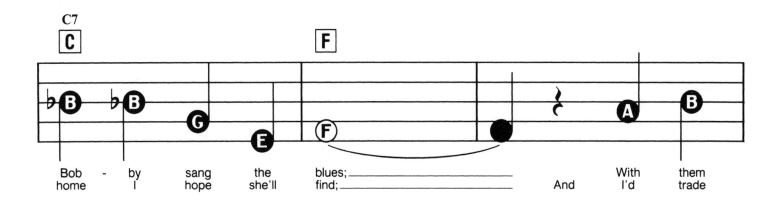

Bob - by sang the blues;_____ And With them
home I hope she'll find;_____ I'd trade

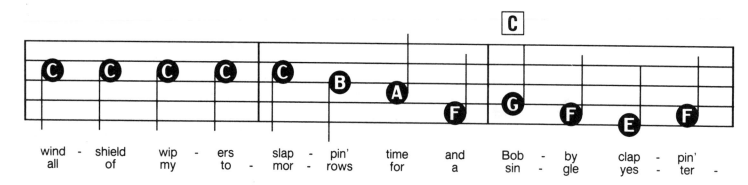

windshield wipers slappin' time and a Bobby clappin'
all of my tomorrows time for a single yester-

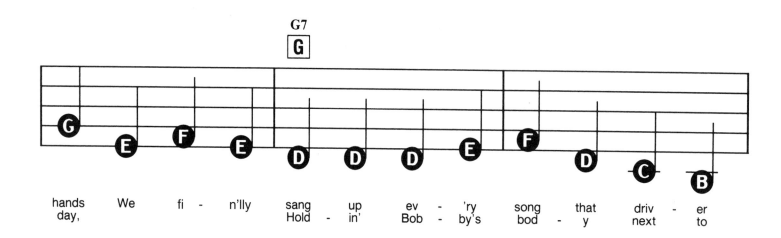

hands We fi-n'lly sang up ev-'ry song that driv-er
day, Hold-in' Bob-by's bod-y next to

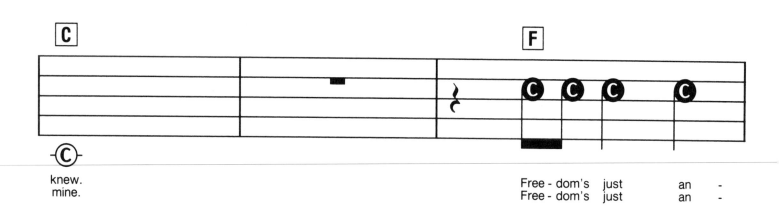

knew.
mine.

Free-dom's just an-
Free-dom's just an-

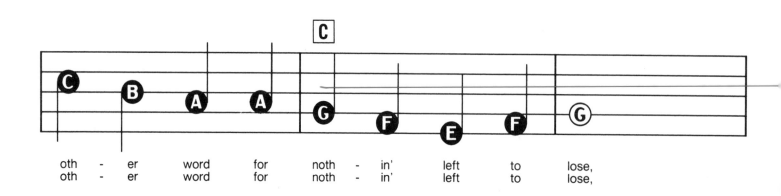

oth-er word for noth-in' left to lose,
oth-er word for noth-in' left to lose,

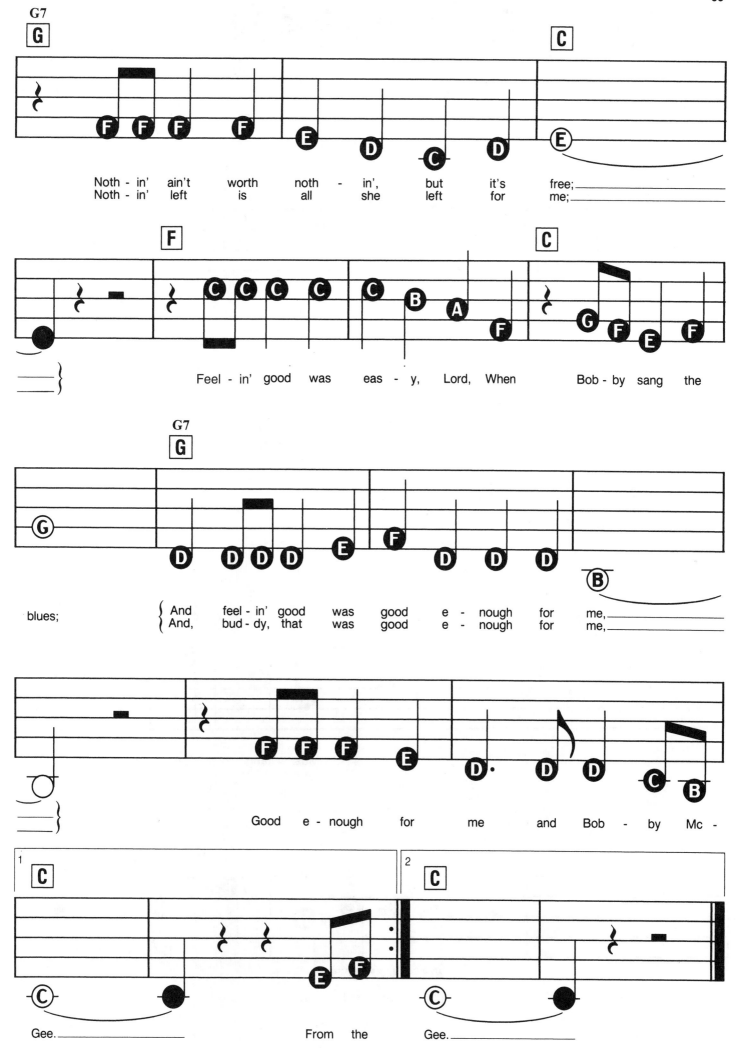

Mustang Sally

Registration 4
Rhythm: Rock or Dance

Words and Music by
Sonny Rice

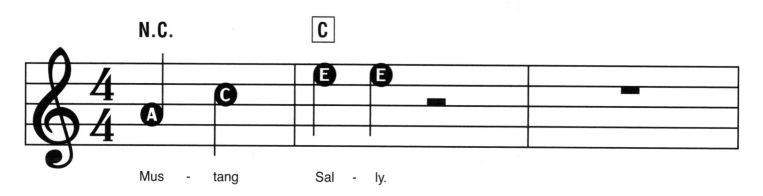

Mus - tang   Sal - ly.

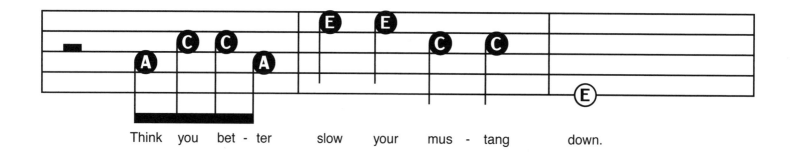

Think you bet - ter   slow   your   mus - tang   down.

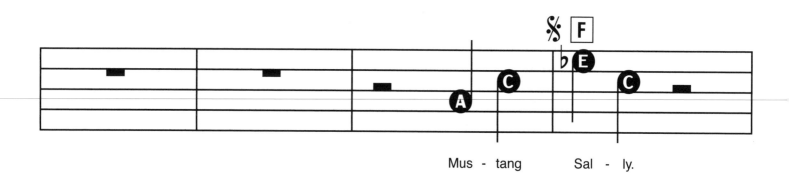

Mus - tang   Sal - ly.

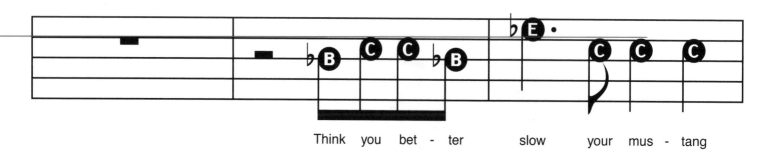

Think you bet - ter   slow   your mus - tang

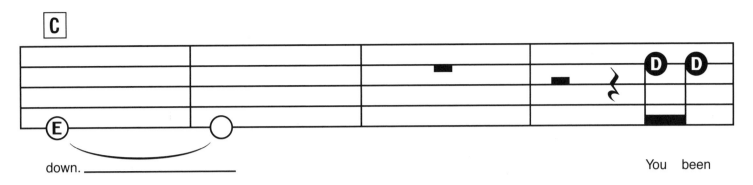

down. _____ You been

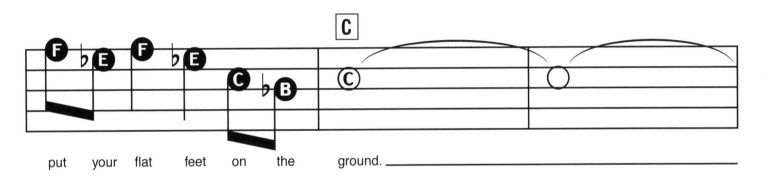

run - ning all o - ver the town now. Oh! I guess I'll have to

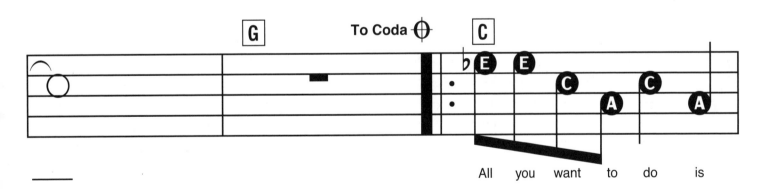

put your flat feet on the ground. _____

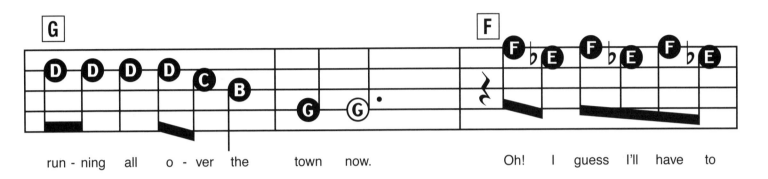

_____ All you want to do is

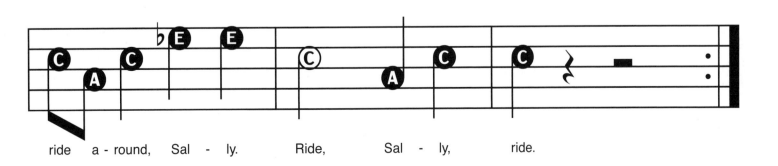

ride a - round, Sal - ly. Ride, Sal - ly, ride.

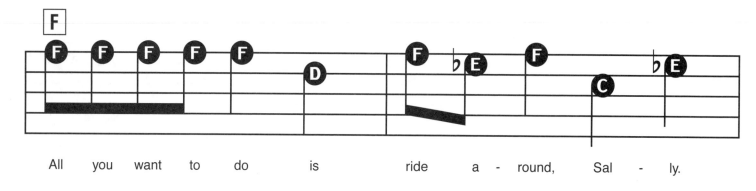

All you want to do is ride a - round, Sal - ly.

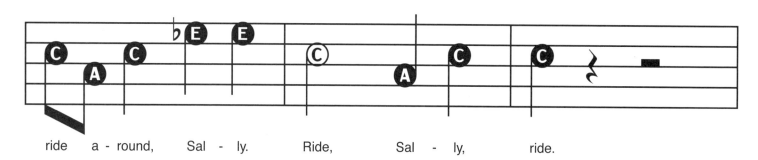

Ride, Sal - ly, ride. All you want to do is

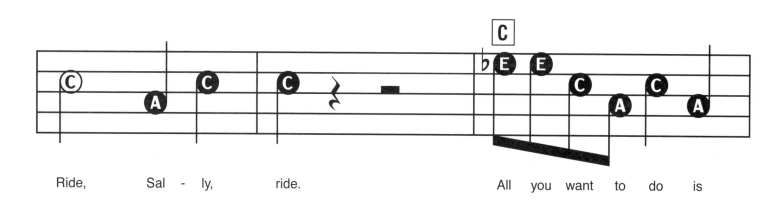

ride a - round, Sal - ly. Ride, Sal - ly, ride.

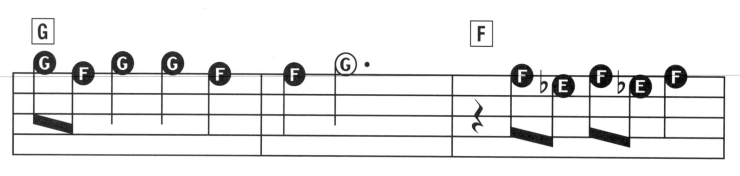

One of these ear - ly morn - ings, oh, you gon - na be

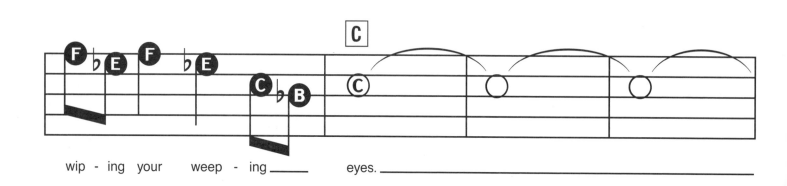

wip - ing your weep - ing _____ eyes. _____

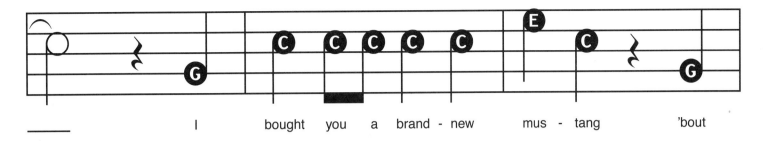

_____ I bought you a brand-new mus-tang 'bout

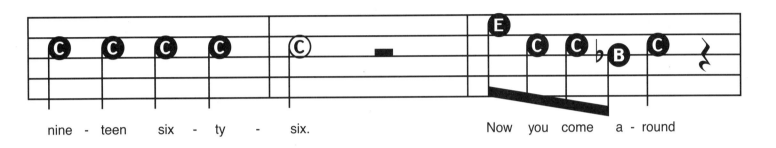

nine-teen six-ty - six. Now you come a-round

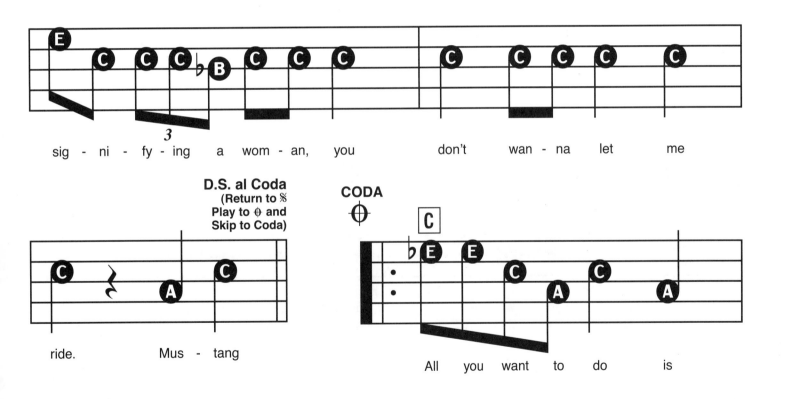

sig-ni-fy-ing a wom-an, you don't wan-na let me

D.S. al Coda
(Return to 𝄋
Play to ⊕ and
Skip to Coda)

CODA

ride. Mus-tang

All you want to do is

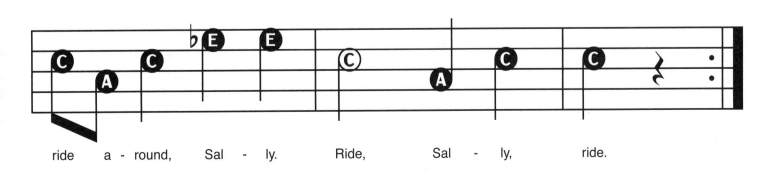

ride a-round, Sal - ly. Ride, Sal - ly, ride.

Old Time Rock & Roll

Registration 8
Rhythm: Rock 'n' Roll

Words and Music by George Jackson
and Thomas E. Jones III

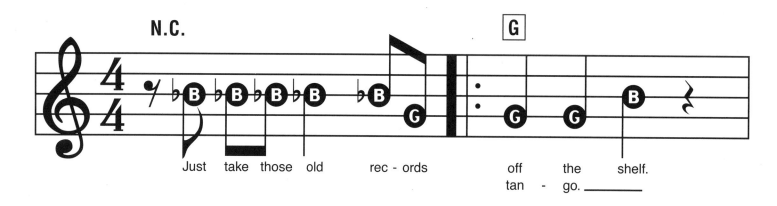

Just take those old rec - ords off the shelf.
tan - go. _____

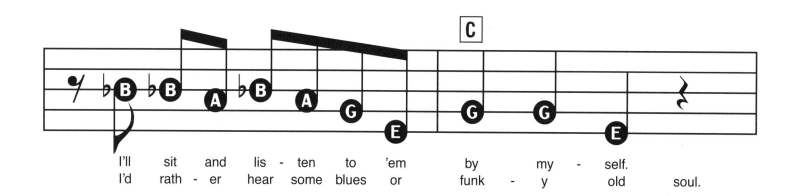

I'll sit and lis - ten to 'em by my - self.
I'd rath - er hear some blues or funk - y old soul.

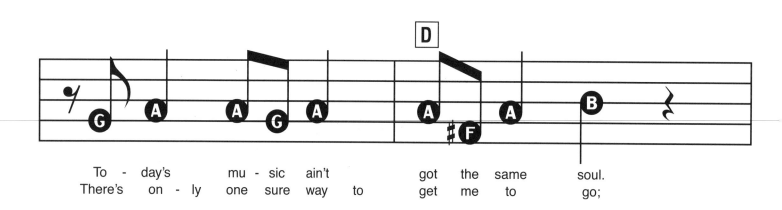

To - day's mu - sic ain't got the same soul.
There's on - ly one sure way to get me to go;

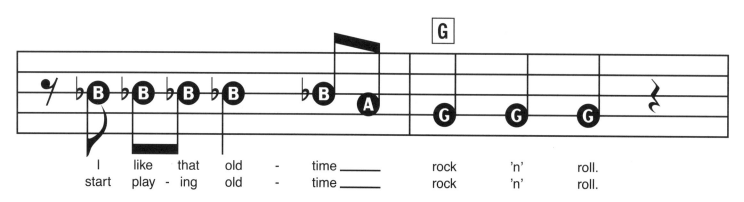

I like that old - time _____ rock 'n' roll.
start play - ing old - time _____ rock 'n' roll.

101

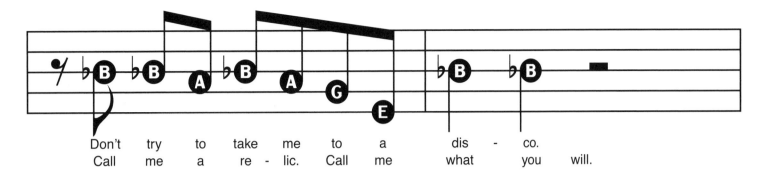

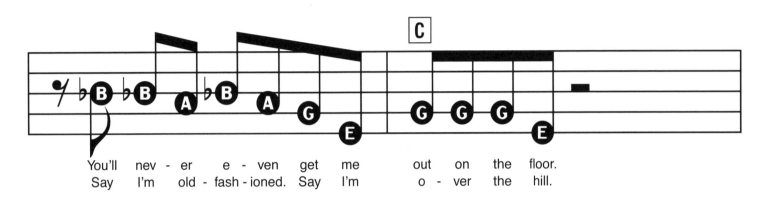

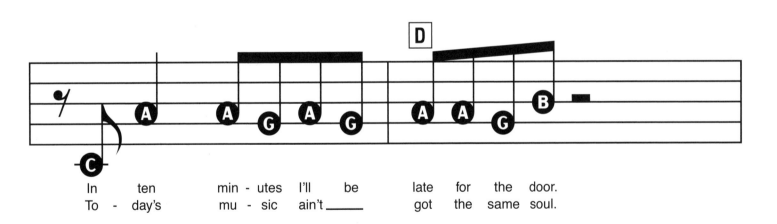

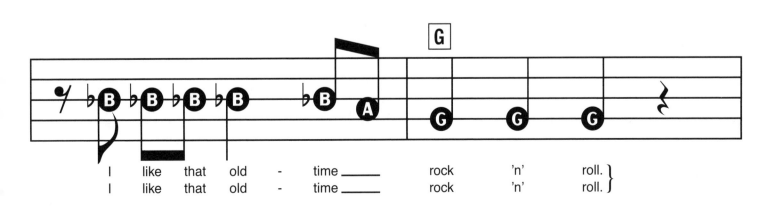

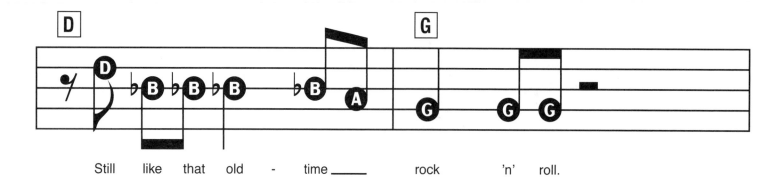

Still   like   that   old - time _____   rock   'n'   roll.

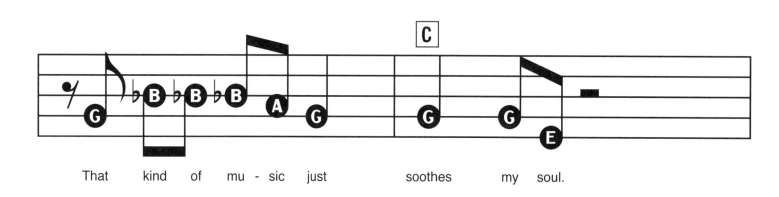

That   kind   of   mu - sic   just   soothes   my   soul.

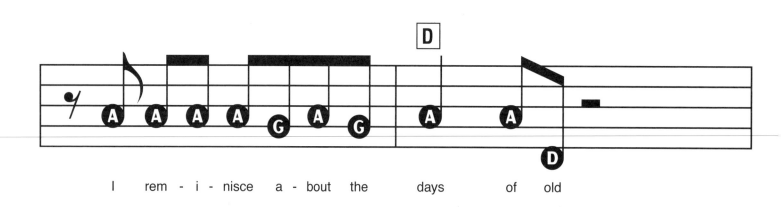

I   rem - i - nisce   a - bout   the   days   of   old

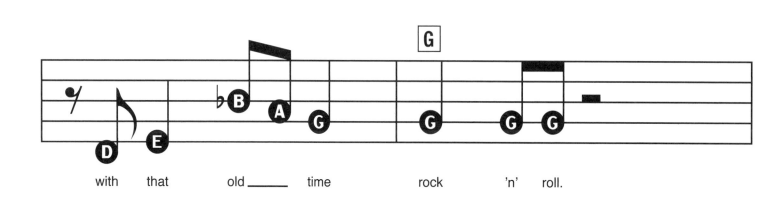

with   that   old _____ time   rock   'n'   roll.

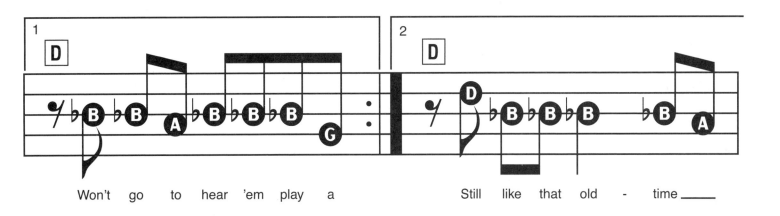

Won't go to hear 'em play a   Still like that old - time _____

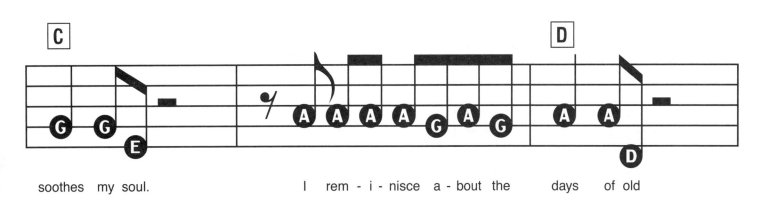

rock 'n' roll.   That kind of mu - sic just

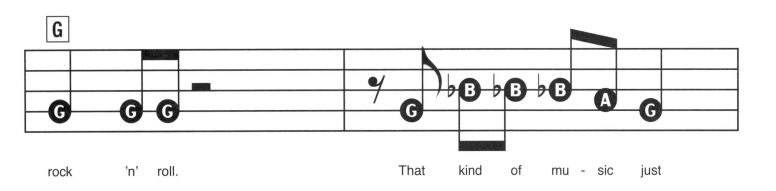

soothes my soul.   I rem - i - nisce a - bout the   days of old

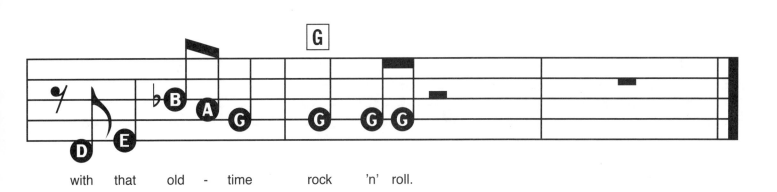

with that old - time   rock 'n' roll.

Ring of Fire

Registration 3
Rhythm: Rock

Words and Music by Merle Kilgore
and June Carter

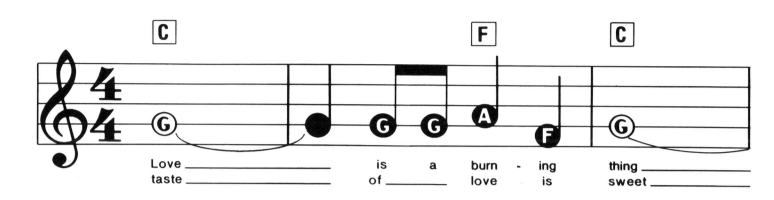

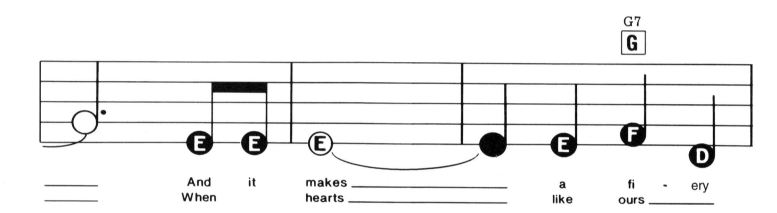

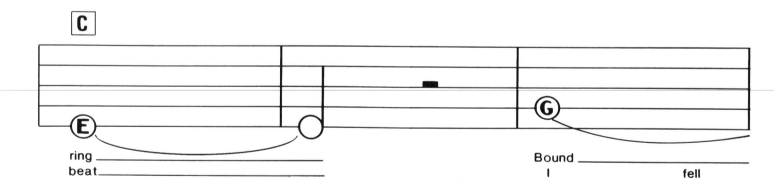

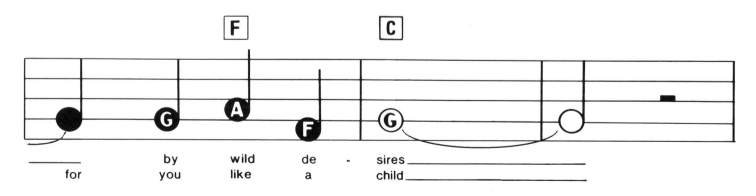

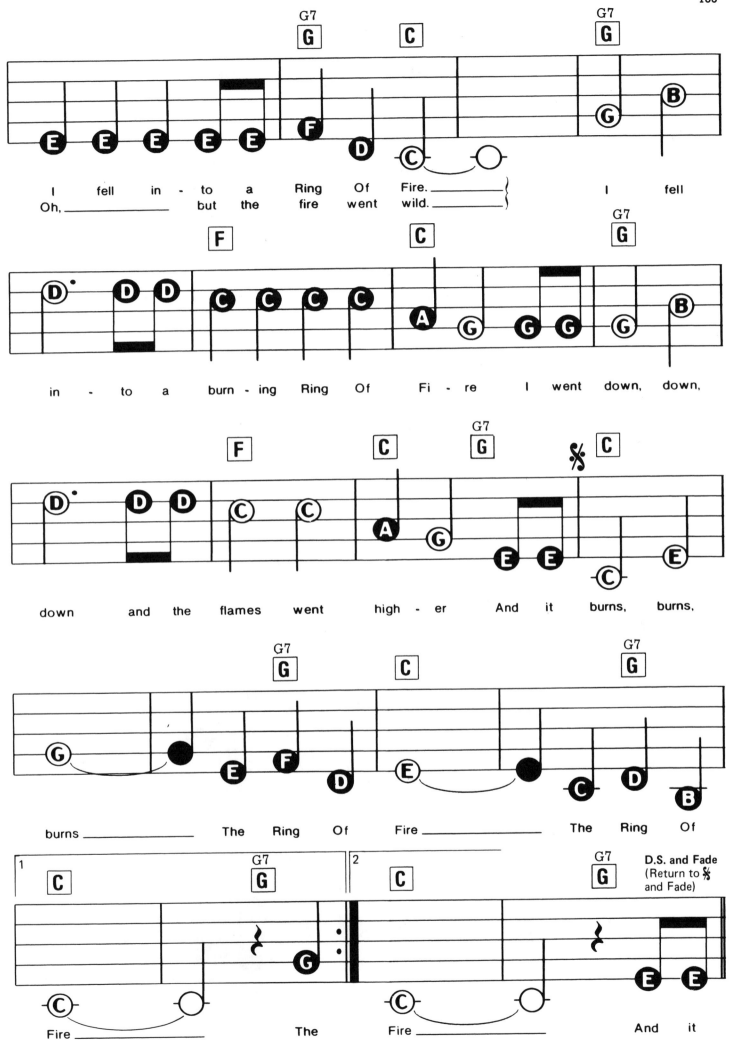

Route 66

Registration 7
Rhythm: Swing

By Bobby Troup

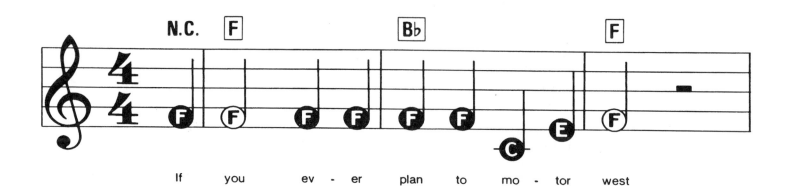

If you ev - er plan to mo - tor west

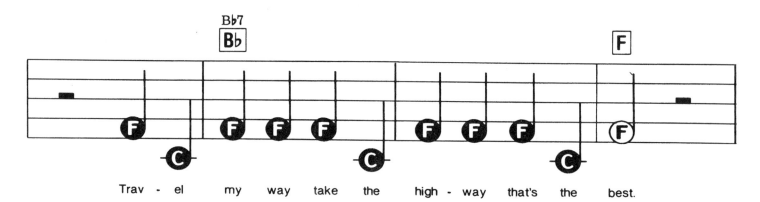

Trav - el my way take the high - way that's the best.

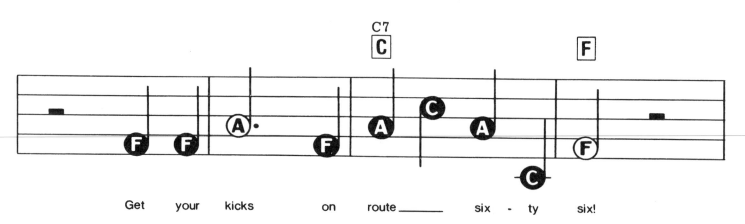

Get your kicks on route _____ six - ty six!

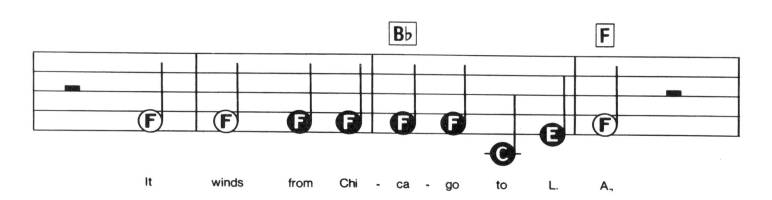

It winds from Chi - ca - go to L. A.,

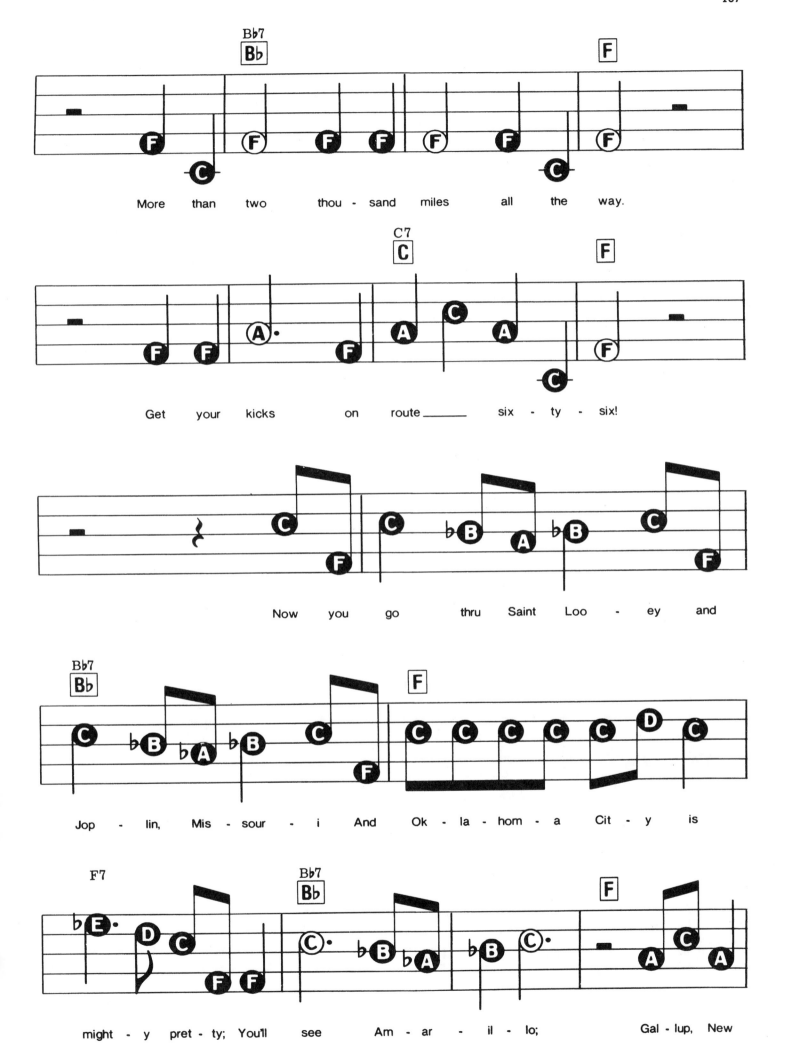

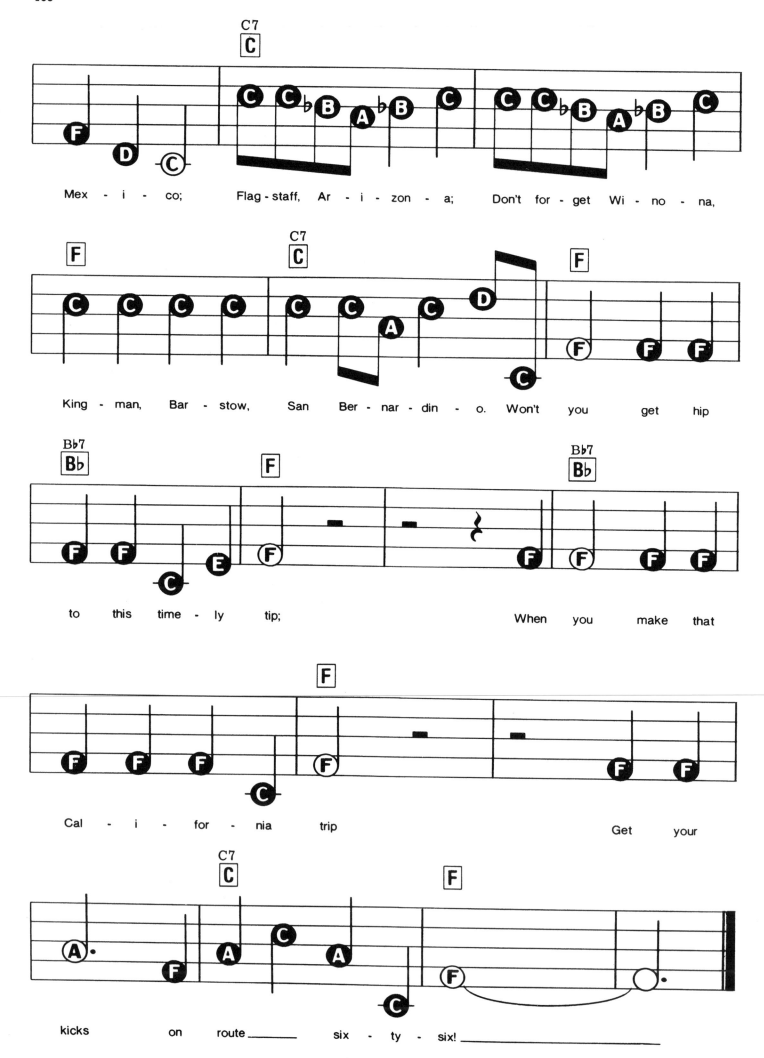

Seven Bridges Road

Registration 8
Rhythm: None

Words and Music by
Stephen T. Young

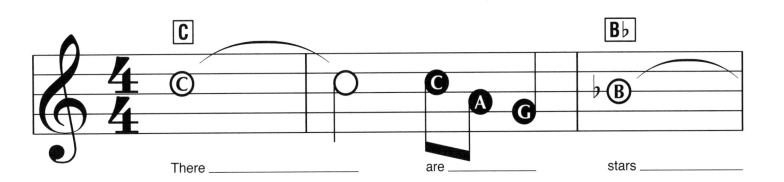

There _____ are _____ stars _____

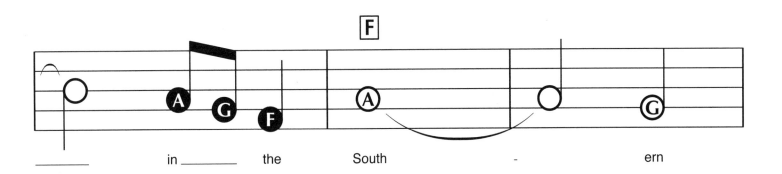

_____ in _____ the South - ern

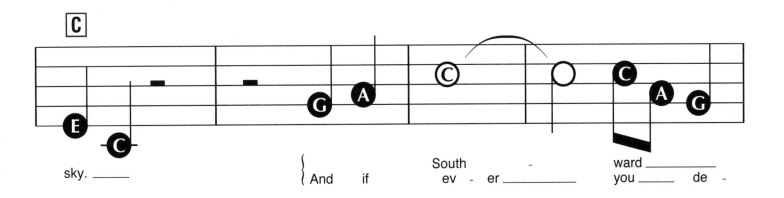

sky. _____ And if ev - er _____ you _____ South - ward _____ you _____ de -

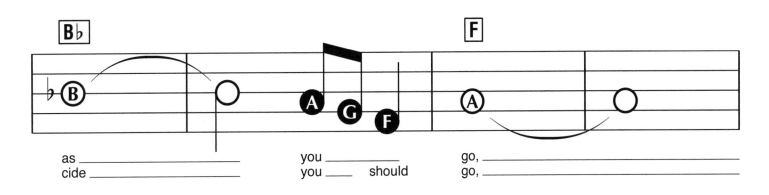

as _____ you _____ go,
cide _____ you _____ should go, _____

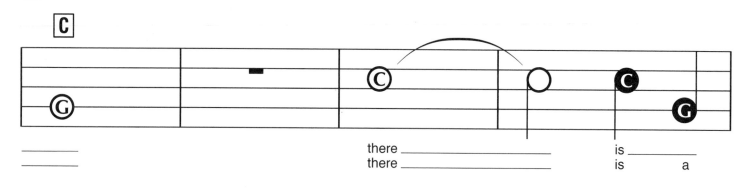

there _____ is _____
there _____ is   a

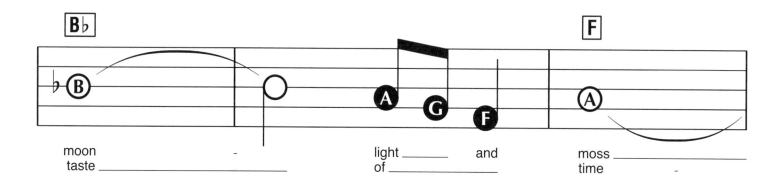

moon   -   light _____ and   moss _____
taste _____   of _____   time   -

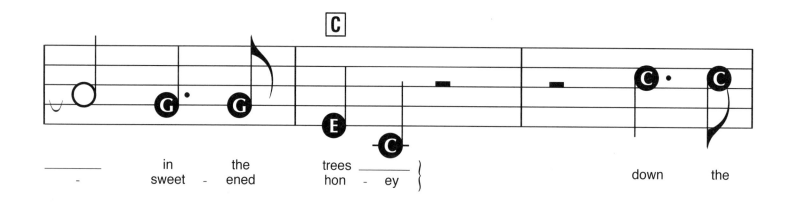

_____   in   the   trees _____   down   the
-        sweet - ened   hon - ey ⎬

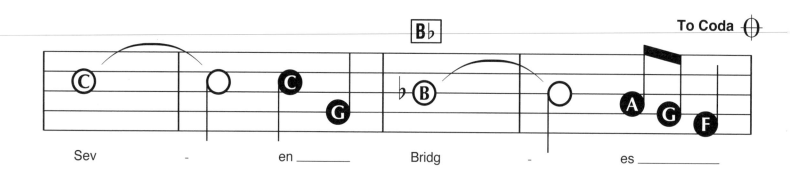

To Coda ⊕

Sev   -   en _____   Bridg   -   es _____

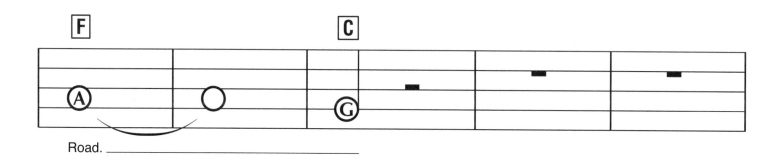

Road. _____

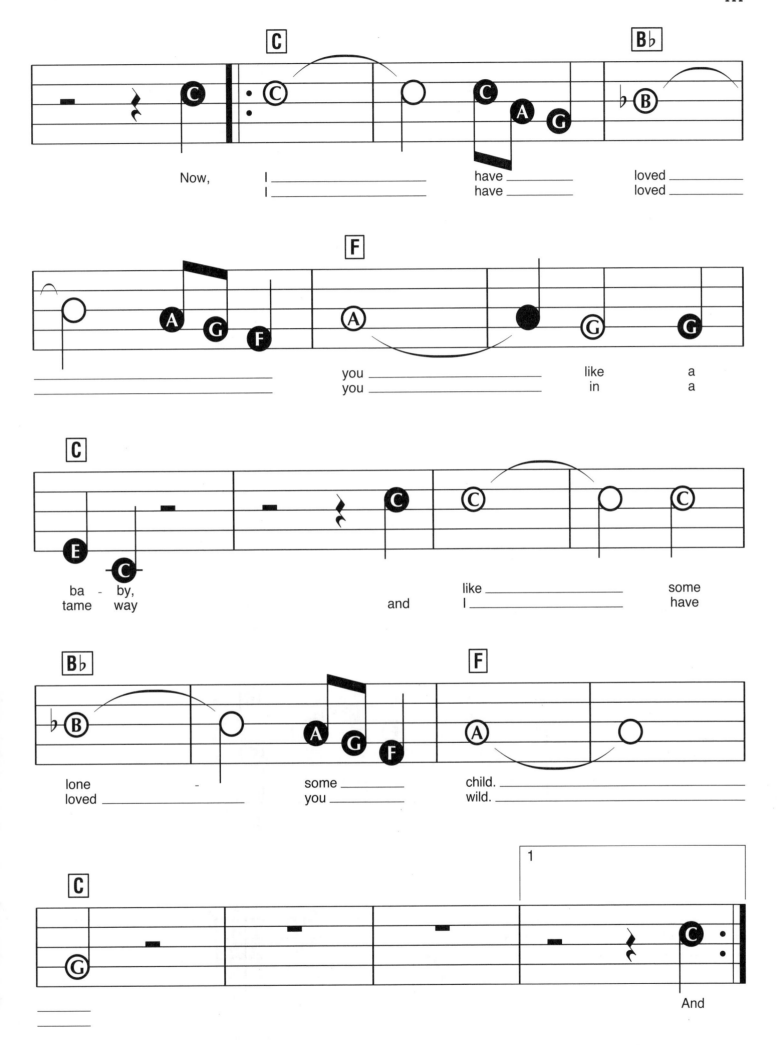

112

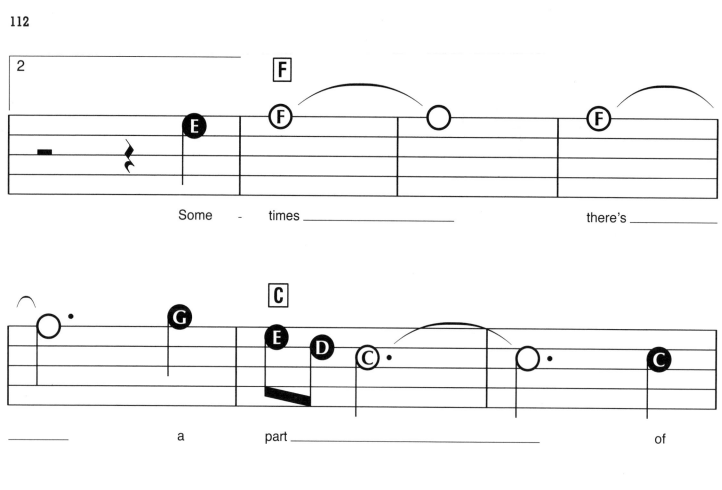

Some - times _____ there's _____

_____ a part _____ of

me has to turn _____ from

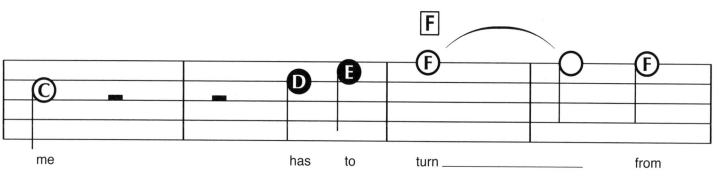

here _____ and go,

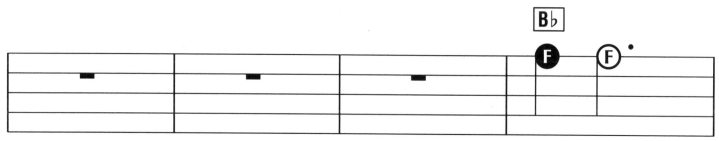

run - ning

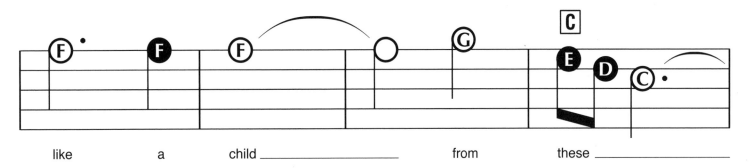

like   a   child _____   from   these _____

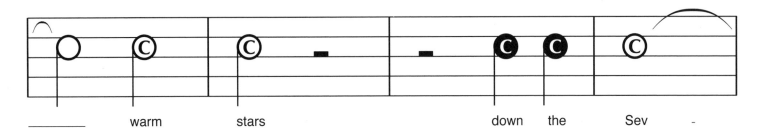

_____   warm   stars   down   the   Sev   -

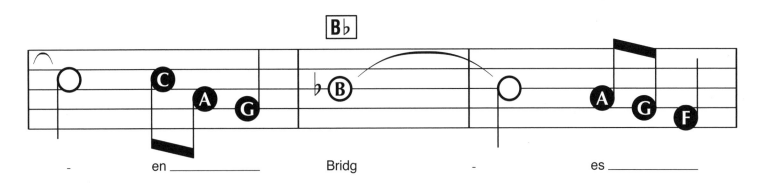

-                en _____   Bridg   -   es _____

D.C. al Coda
(Return to beginning
Play to ⊕ and
Skip to Coda)

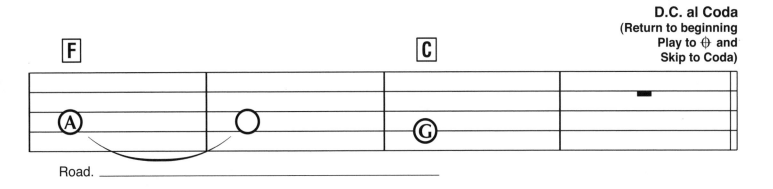

Road. _____

CODA

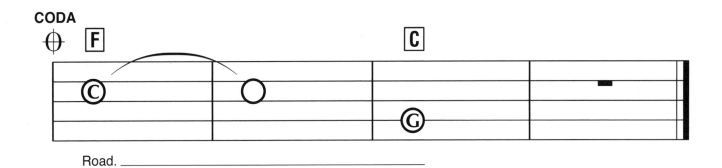

Road. _____

Royals

Registration 9
Rhythm: 8-Beat or Calypso

Words and Music by Ella Yelich-O'Connor
and Joel Little

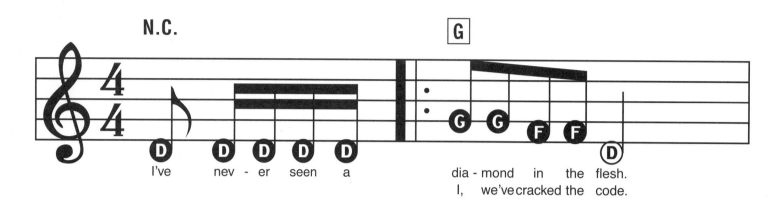

I've nev-er seen a dia-mond in the flesh.
I, we've cracked the code.

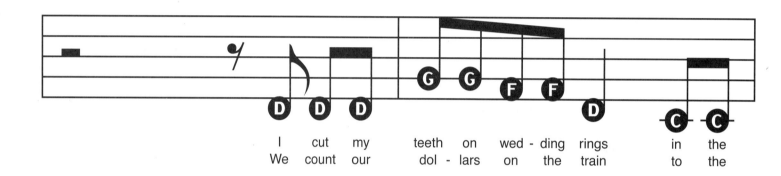

I cut my teeth on wed-ding rings in the
We count our dol-lars on the train to the

mov-ies. And I'm not proud of my ad-dress.
par-ty. And ev-'ry-one who knows us knows

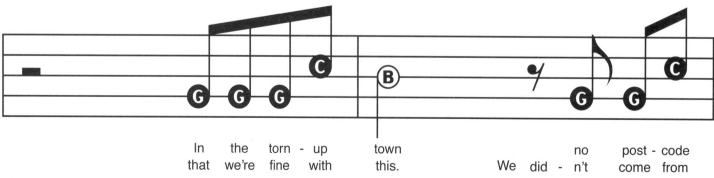

In the torn-up town this. no post-code
that we're fine with We did-n't come from

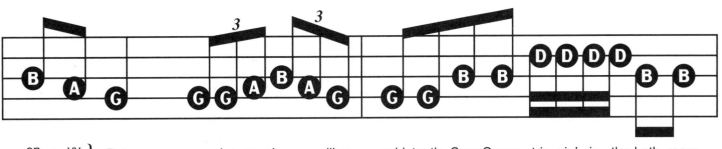

en - vy. 〉 But   ev - 'ry song's ____ like: gold teeth, Grey Goose, trip-pin' in the bath-room,
mon - ey. 〉

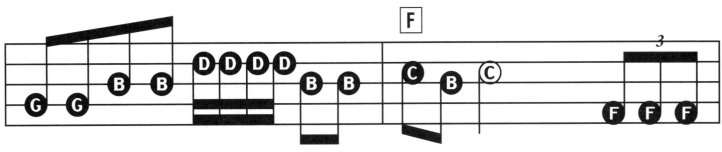

blood stains, ball - gowns, trash-in' the ho - tel room.   We   don't care,   we're driv - in'

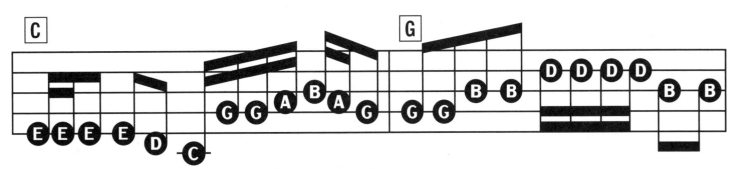

Cad - il - lacs   in   our dreams. But ev - 'ry - bod-y's like: Cris - tal, May - bach, dia-monds on your time - piece,

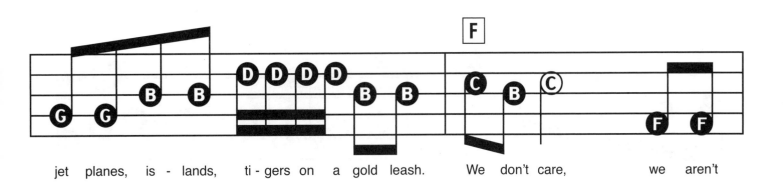

jet planes, is - lands,   ti - gers on   a gold leash.   We   don't care,   we   aren't

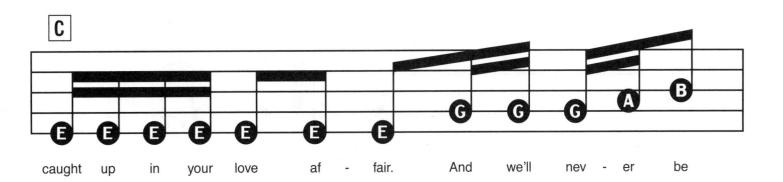

caught up   in   your   love   af - fair.   And   we'll   nev - er   be

116

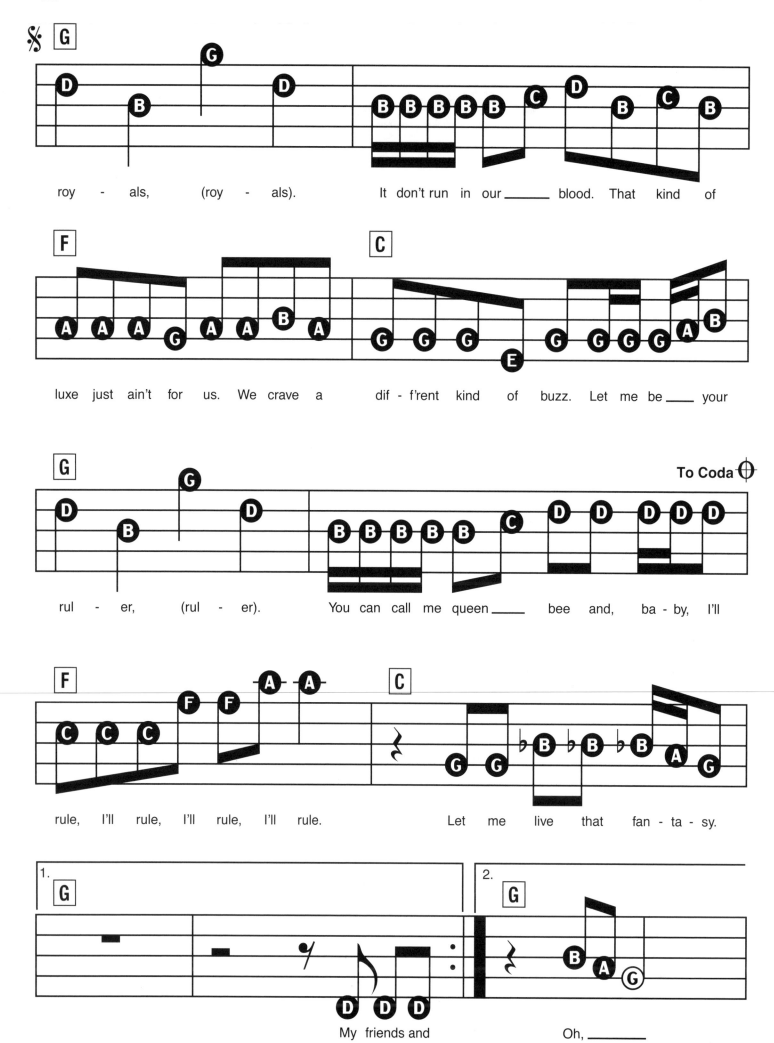

117

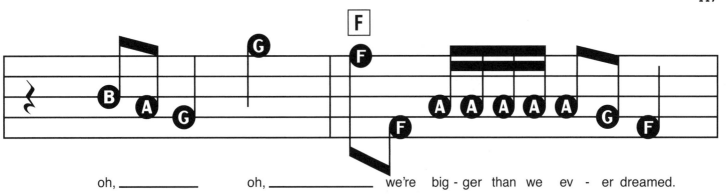

oh, _____ oh, _____ we're big - ger than we ev - er dreamed.

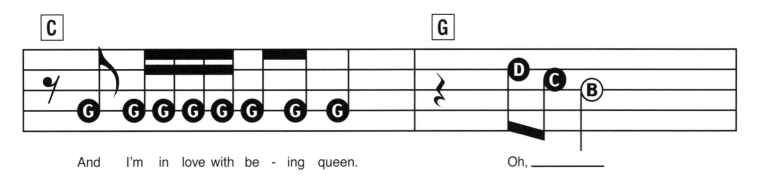

And I'm in love with be - ing queen. Oh, _____

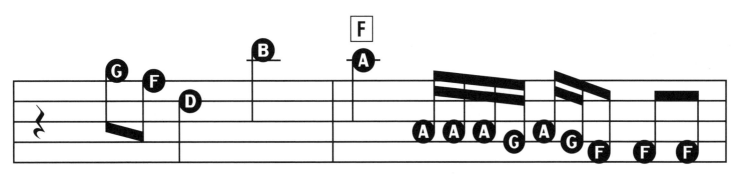

oh, _____ oh, _____ life is game with - out a care. We aren't

D.S. al Coda
(Return to 𝄋
Play to ⊕ and
Skip to Coda)

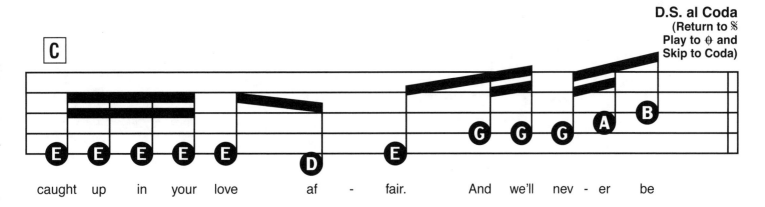

caught up in your love af - fair. And we'll nev - er be

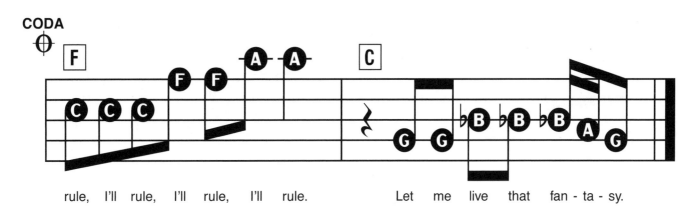

rule, I'll rule, I'll rule, I'll rule. Let me live that fan - ta - sy.

Sad Songs
(Say So Much)

Registration 2
Rhythm: 8-Beat or Rock

Words and Music by Elton John
and Bernie Taupin

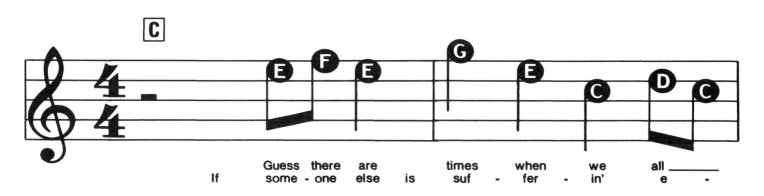

If
Guess there are   times when   we   all _____

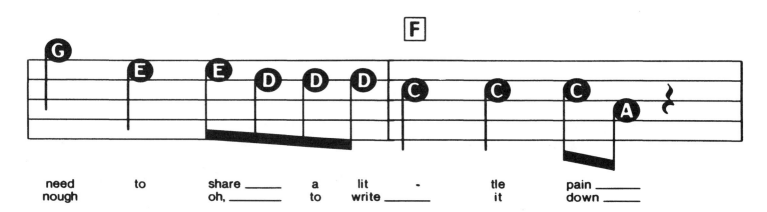

need   to   share _____ a   lit - tle   pain _____
nough   oh, _____ to   write _____   it   down _____

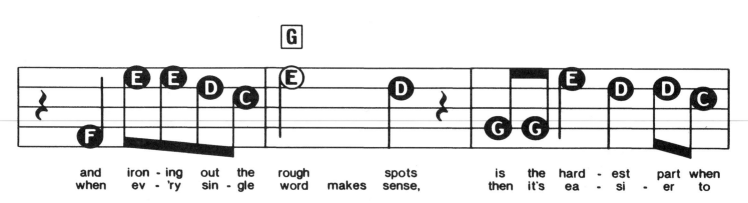

and   iron - ing   out the   rough   spots   is   the hard - est   part when
when   ev - 'ry   sin - gle   word   makes   sense,   then it's ea - si - er   to

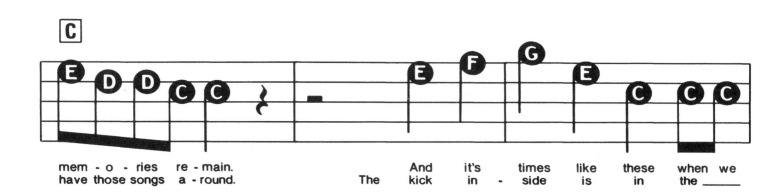

mem - o - ries   re - main.   The   And it's   times   like   these   when we
have those songs a - round.   kick   in - side   is   in the _____

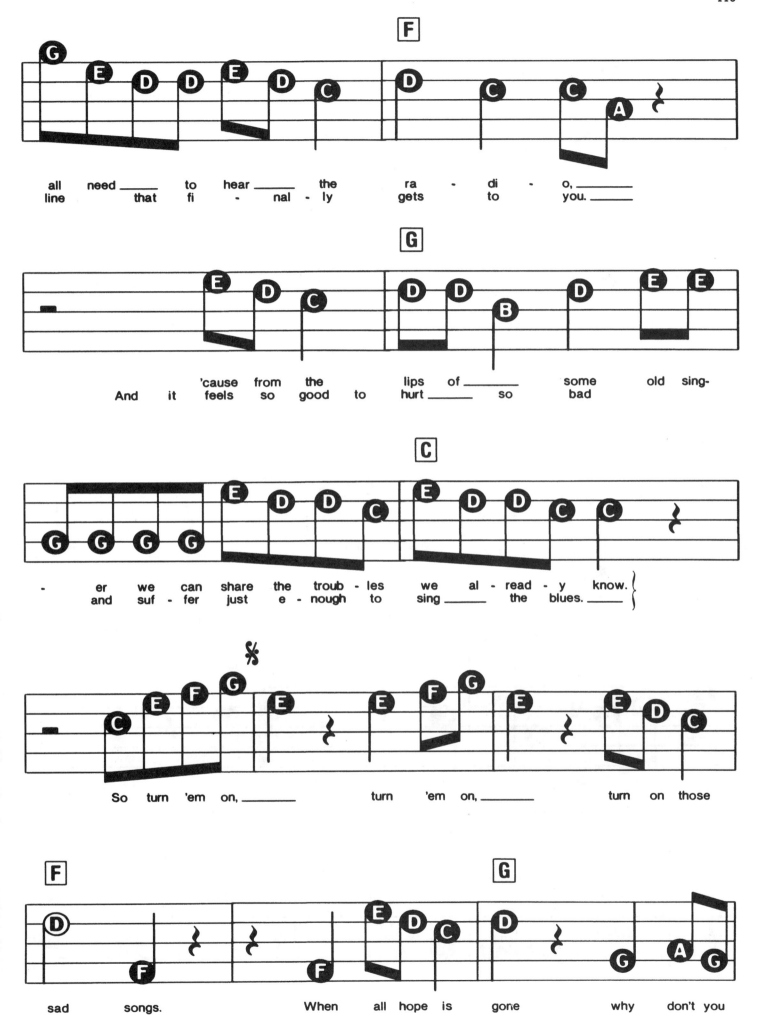

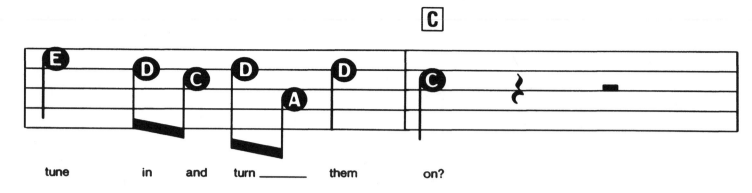

tune   in   and   turn _____ them   on?

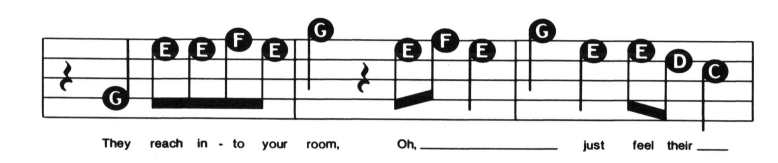

They   reach   in - to   your   room,   Oh, _____ just   feel   their _____

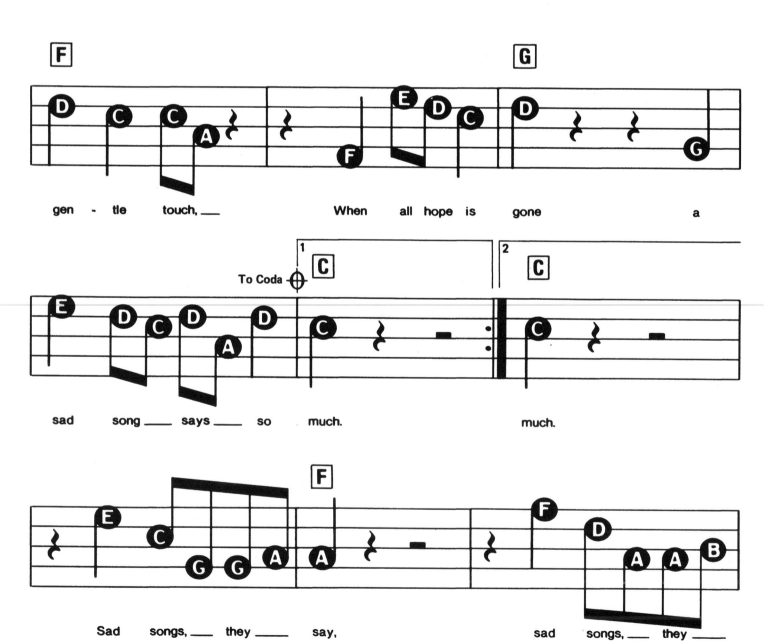

gen - tle   touch, ___   When   all   hope   is   gone   a

sad   song ___ says ___ so   much.   much.

Sad   songs, ___ they ___ say,   sad   songs, ___ they ___

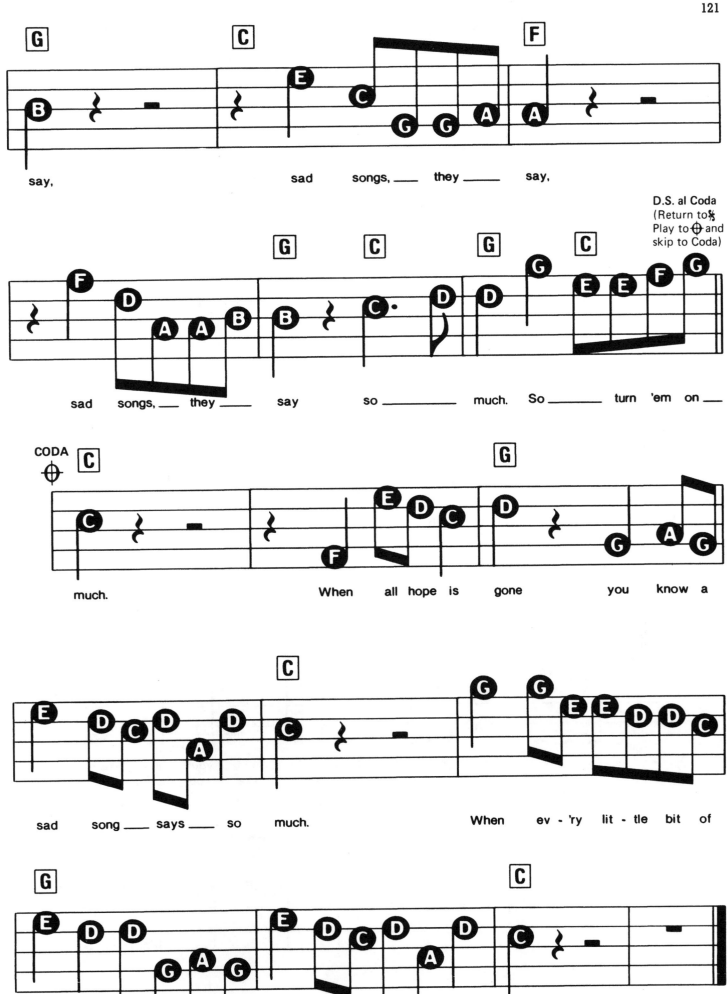

Save the Last Dance for Me

Registration 3
Rhythm: Fox Trot

Words and Music by Doc Pomus
and Mort Shuman

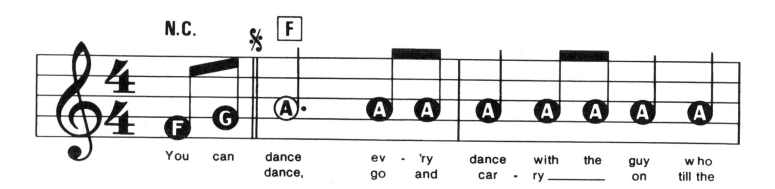

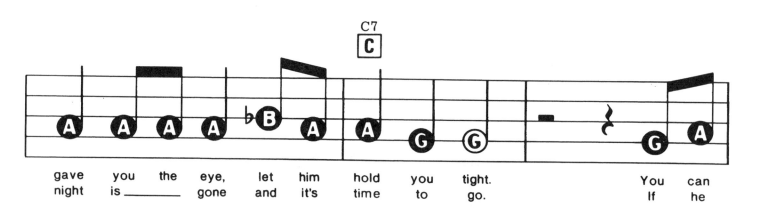

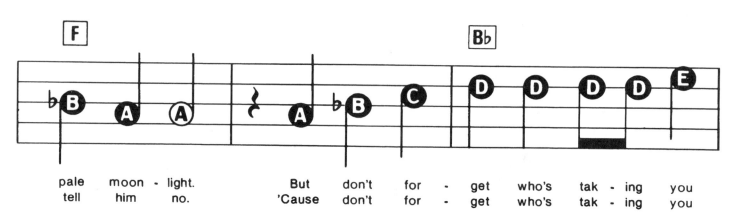

Shake It Off

Registration 9
Rhythm: Pop or Dance

Words and Music by Taylor Swift,
Max Martin and Shellback

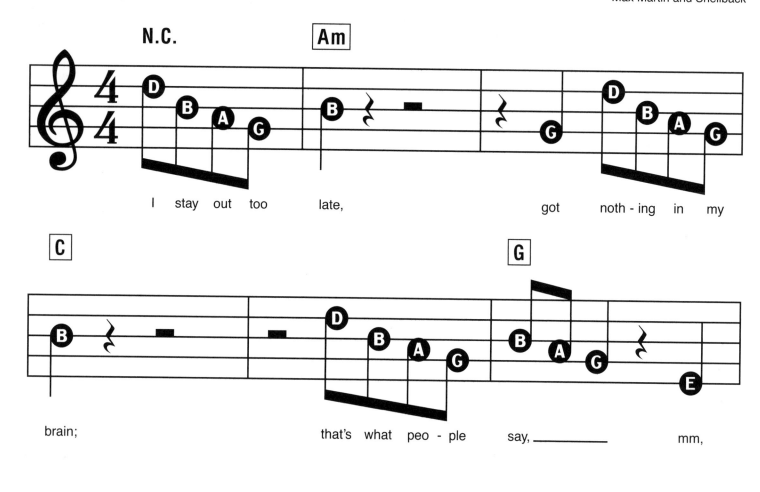

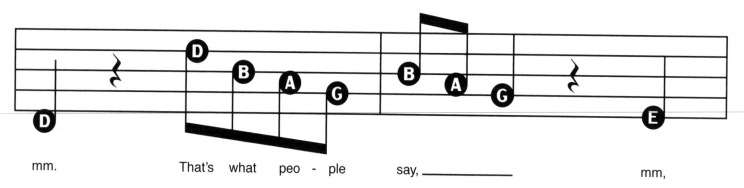

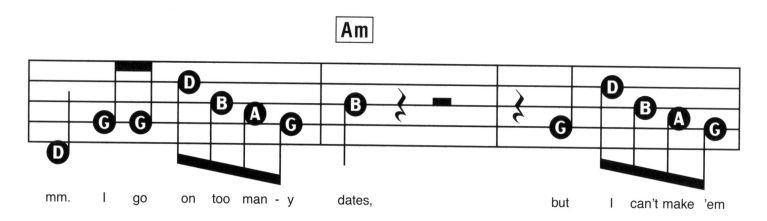

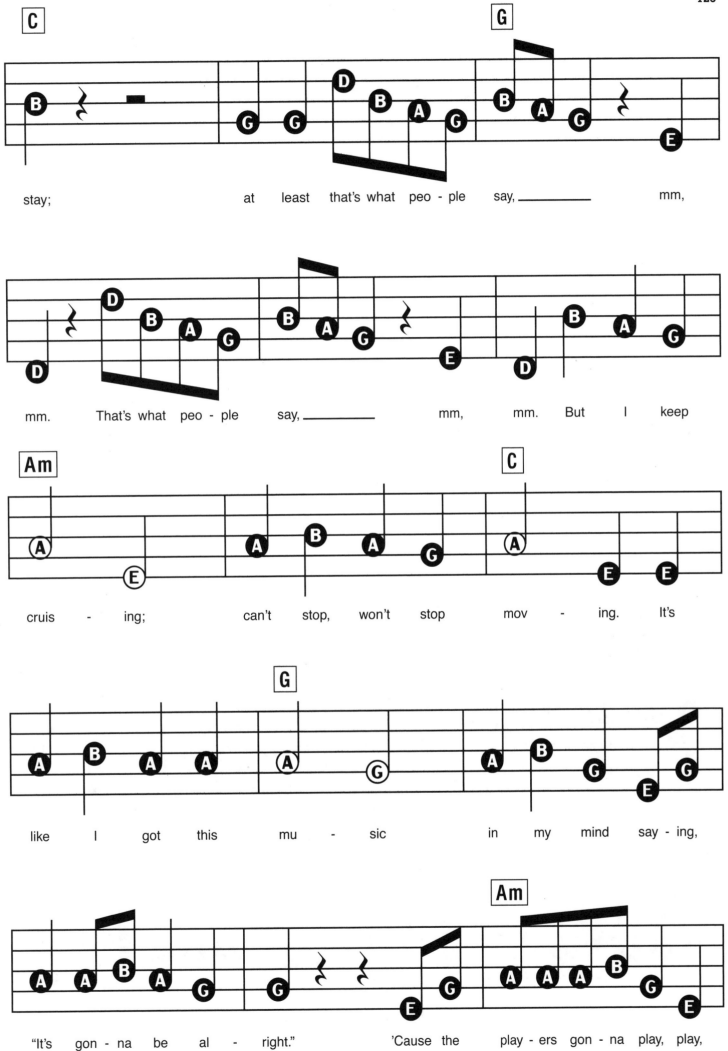

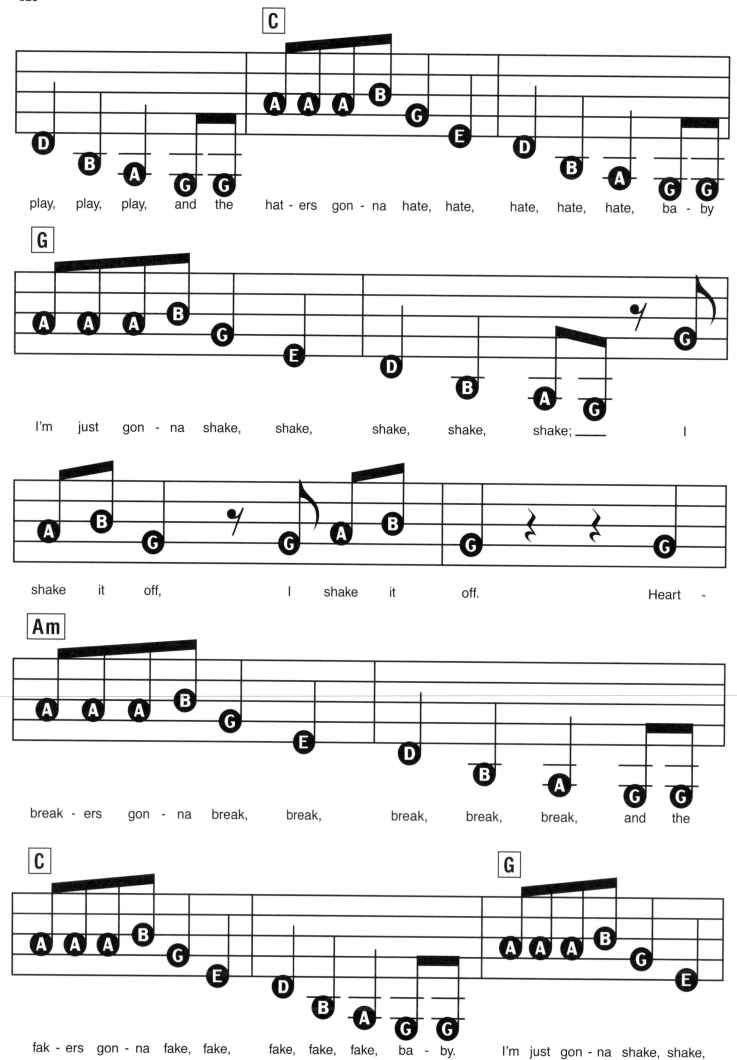

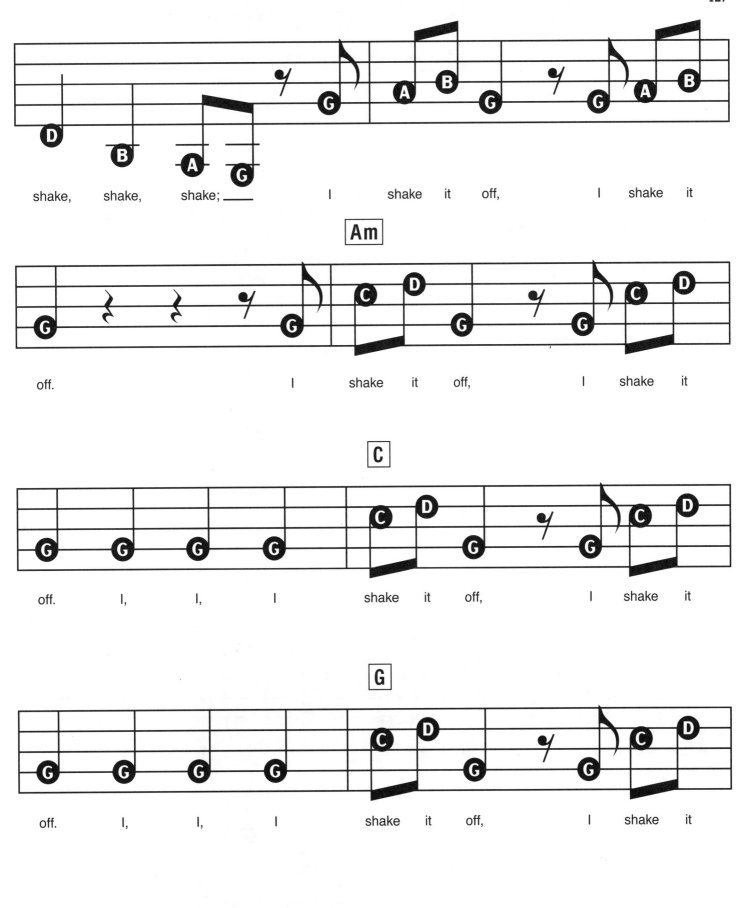

shake, shake, shake;___ I shake it off, I shake it

Am

off. I shake it off, I shake it

C

off. I, I, I shake it off, I shake it

G

off. I, I, I shake it off, I shake it

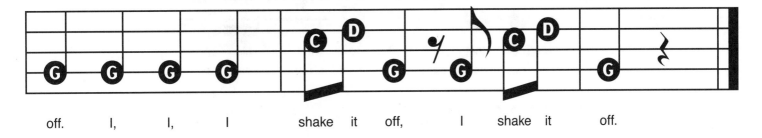

off. I, I, I shake it off, I shake it off.

Signed, Sealed, Delivered I'm Yours

Registration 7
Rhythm: Rock or 8-Beat

Words and Music by Stevie Wonder, Syreeta Wright,
Lee Garrett and Lula Mae Hardaway

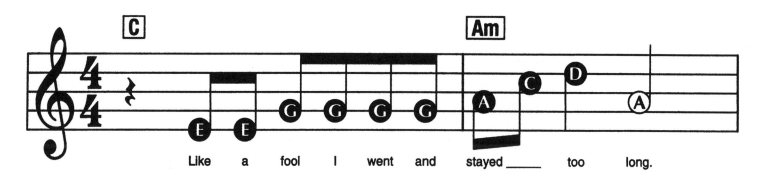

Like a fool I went and stayed _____ too long.

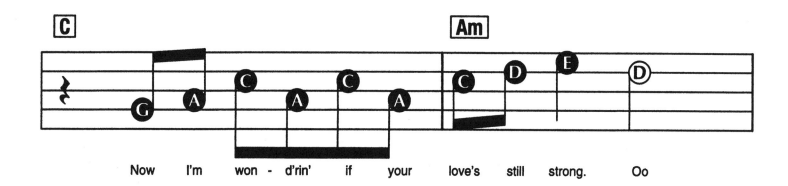

Now I'm won - d'rin' if your love's still strong. Oo

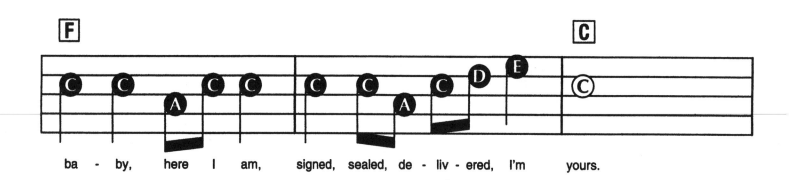

ba - by, here I am, signed, sealed, de - liv - ered, I'm yours.

Then that time I went and said good - bye, _____
Oo - wee, babe you set my soul on fire. _____

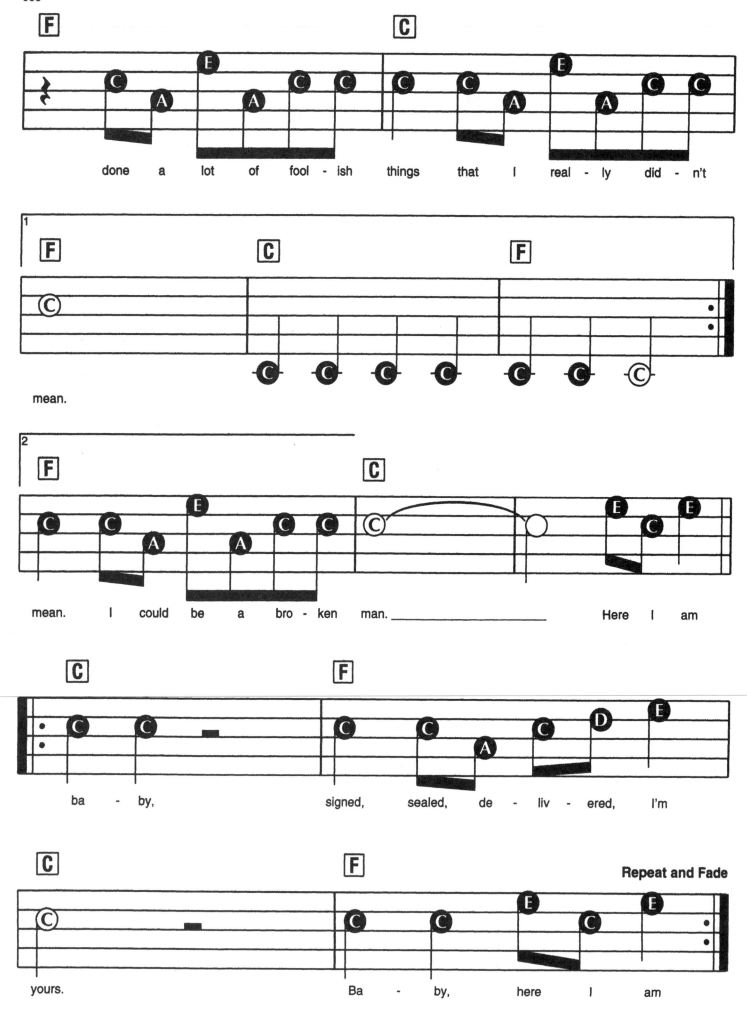

Stir It Up

Registration 2
Rhythm: Reggae or Calypso

Words and Music by
Bob Marley

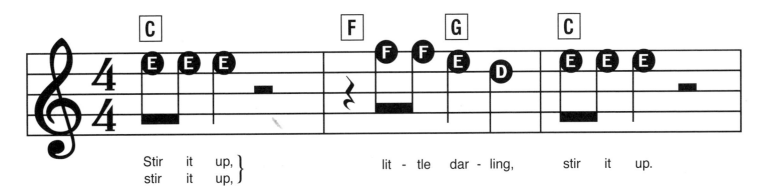

Stir it up,
stir it up, } lit - tle dar - ling, stir it up.

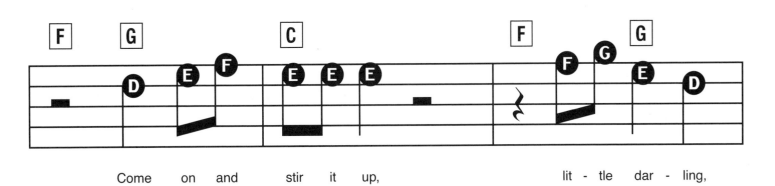

Come on and stir it up, lit - tle dar - ling,

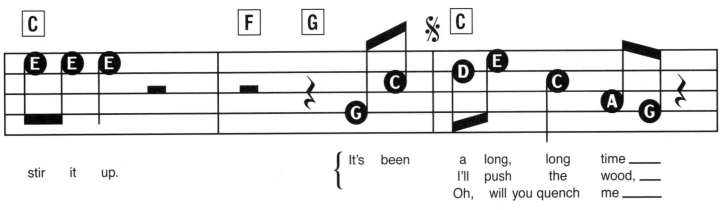

stir it up.

{ It's been a long, long time _____
  I'll push the wood, _____
  Oh, will you quench me _____

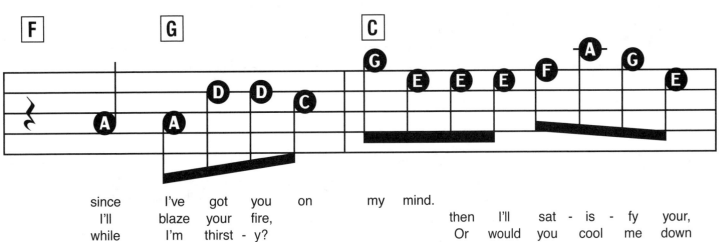

since I've got you on my mind. then I'll sat - is - fy your,
I'll blaze your fire,
while I'm thirst - y? Or would you cool me down

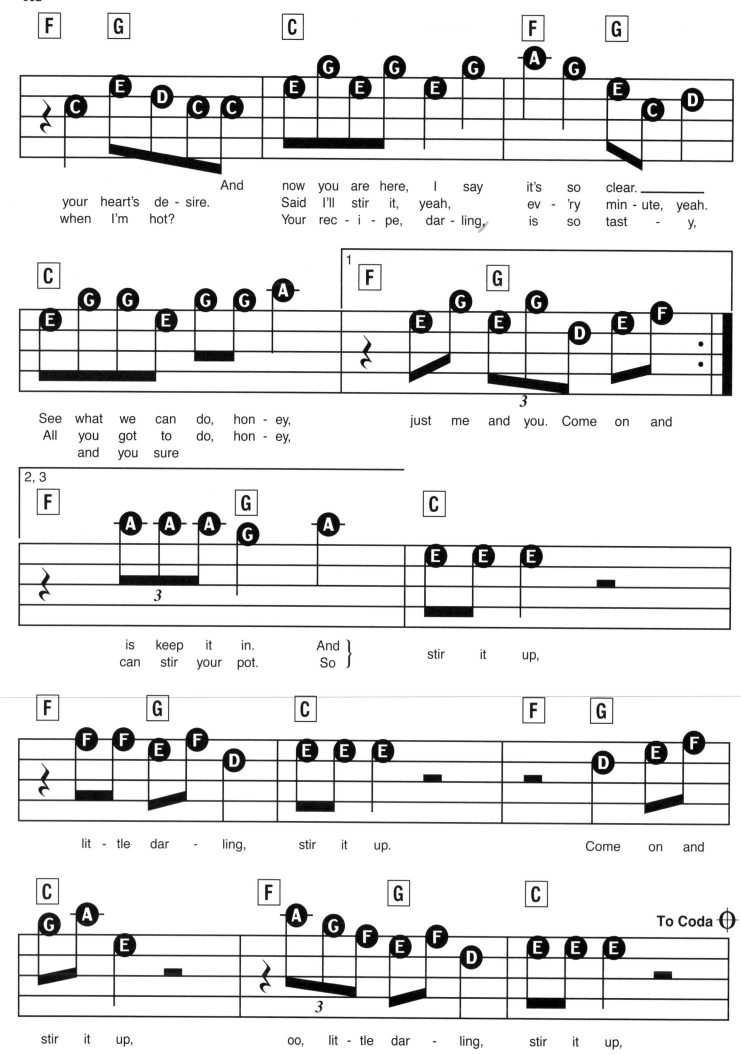

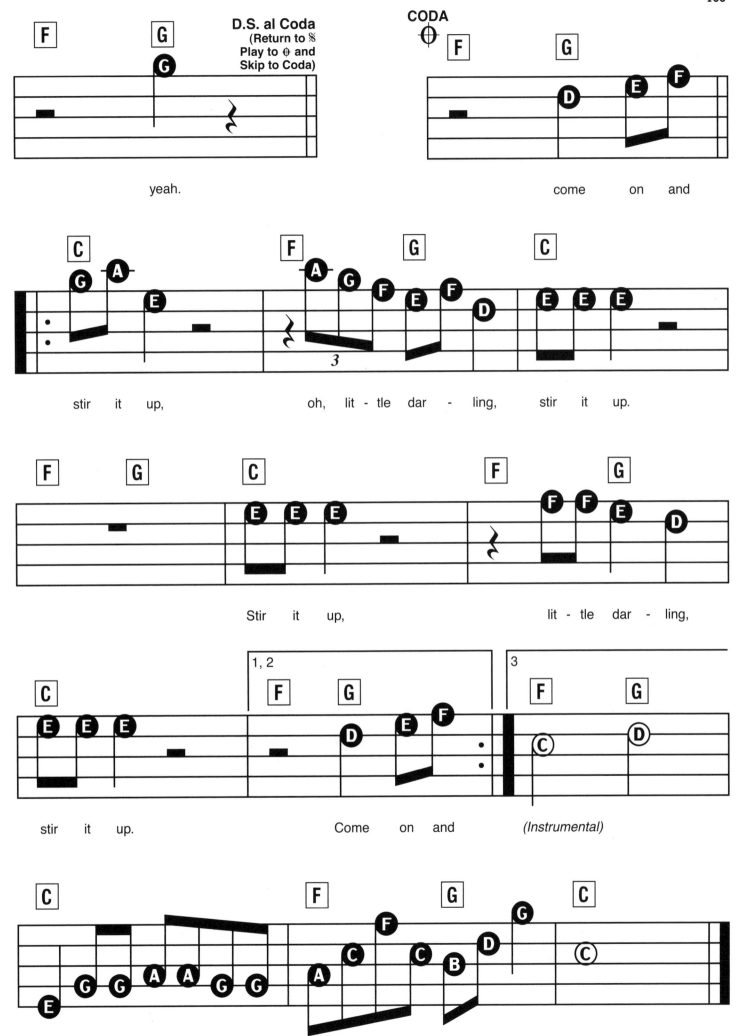

Sugar, Sugar

Registration 1
Rhythm: Rock

Words and Music by Andy Kim
and Jeff Barry

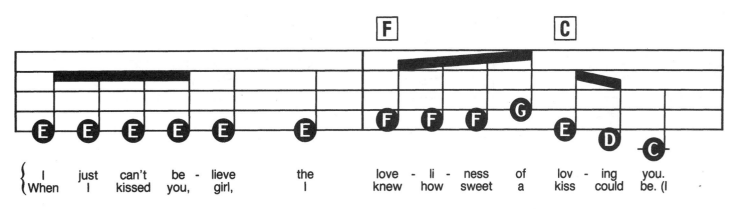

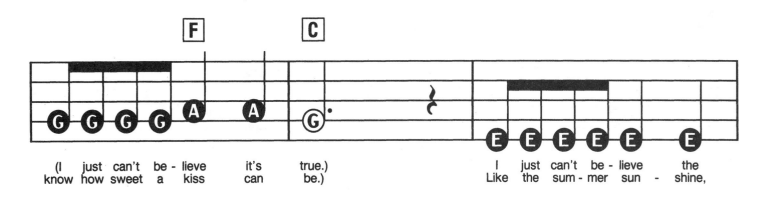

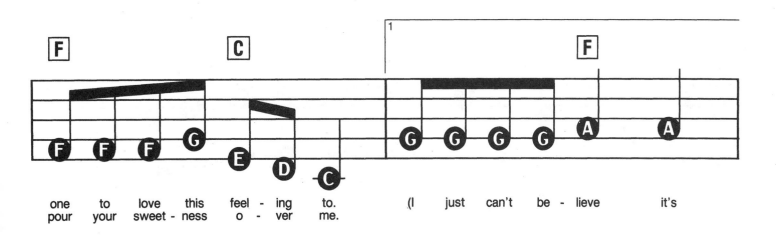

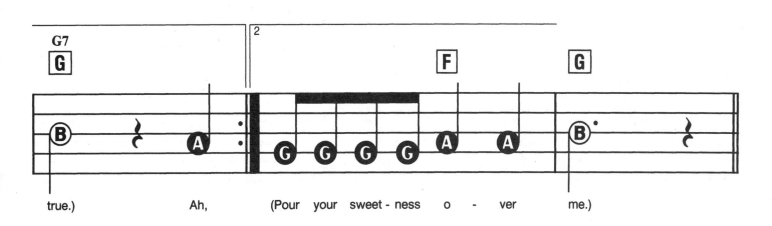

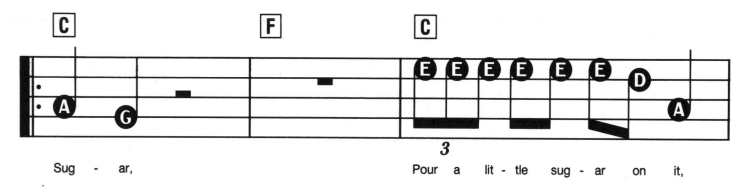

Sug - ar,   Pour a lit - tle sug - ar on it,

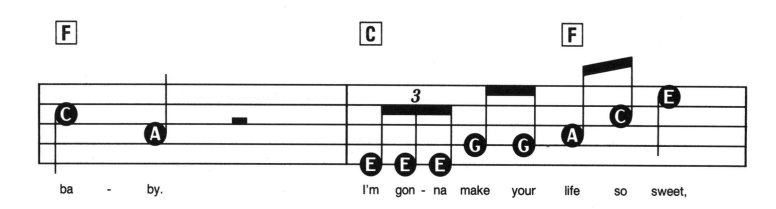

ba - by.   I'm gon - na make your life so sweet,

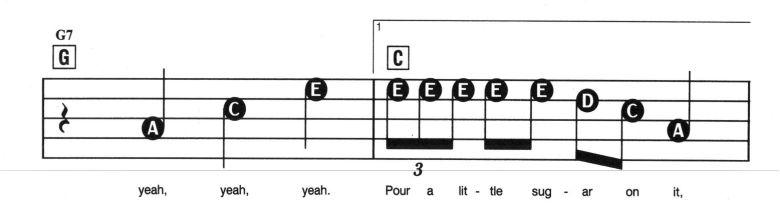

yeah,   yeah,   yeah.   Pour a lit - tle sug - ar on it,

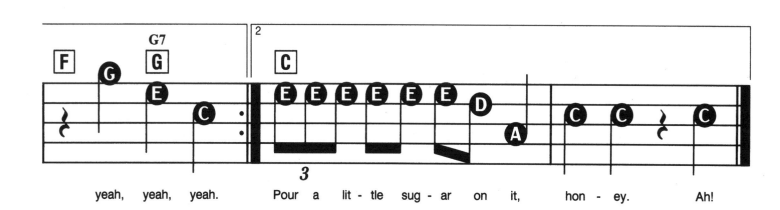

yeah, yeah, yeah.   Pour a lit - tle sug - ar on it, hon - ey.   Ah!

Sweet Caroline

Registration 2
Rhythm: Swing or Fox Trot

Words and Music by
Neil Diamond

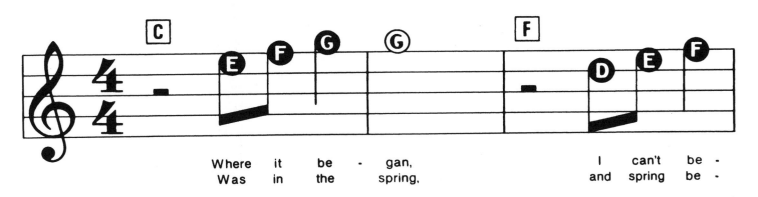

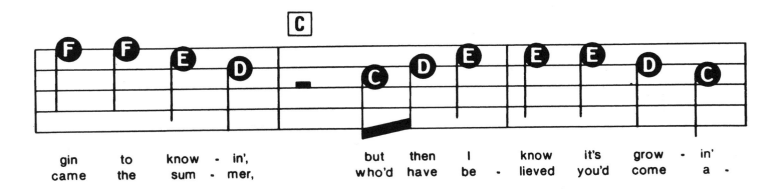

Where it be - gan,
Was in the spring,
I can't be -
and spring be -

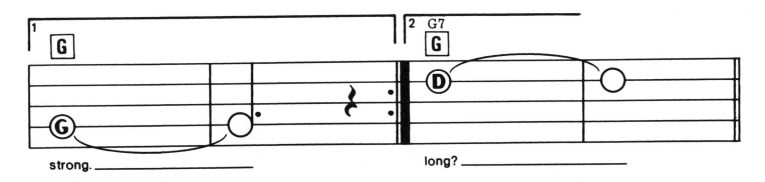

gin to know - in',
came the sum - mer,
but then I know it's grow - in'
who'd have be - lieved you'd come a -

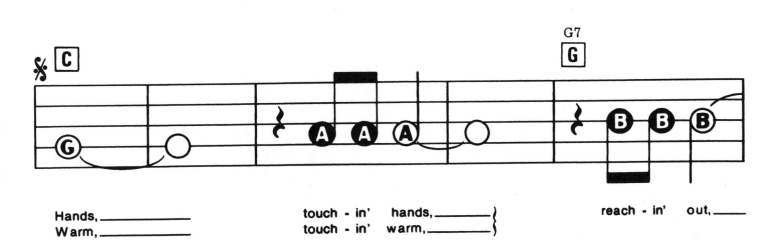

strong. _____
long? _____

Hands, _____
Warm, _____
touch - in' hands, _____
touch - in' warm, _____
reach - in' out, _____

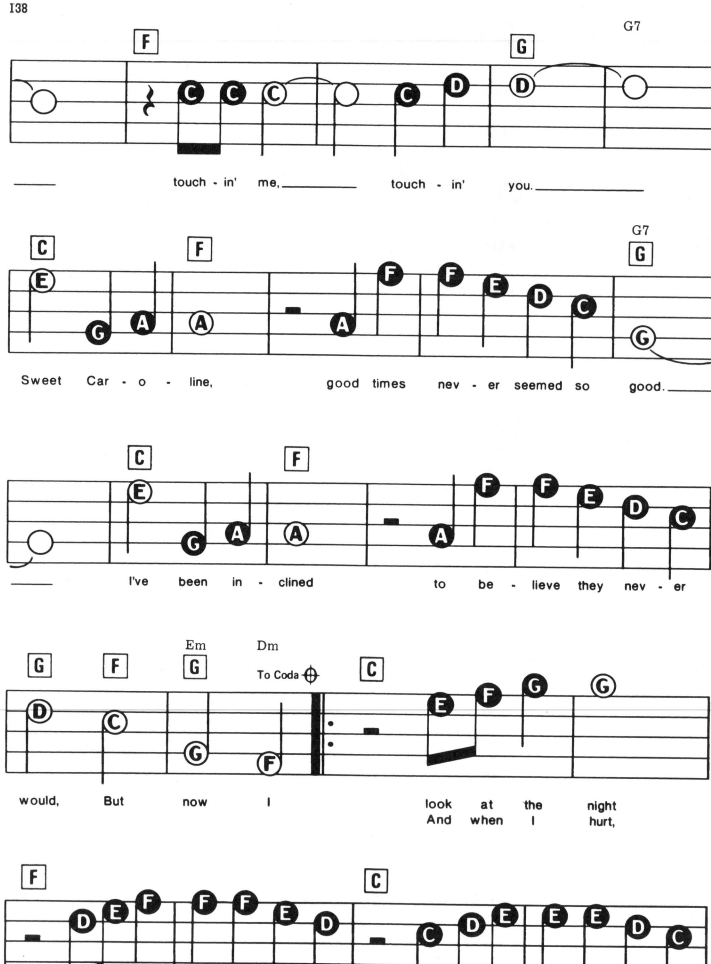

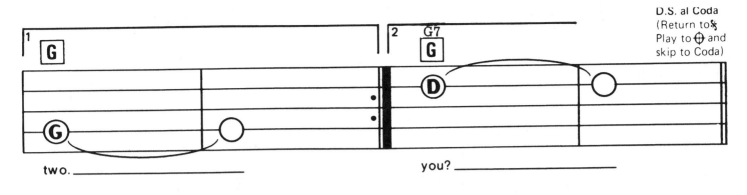

D.S. al Coda
(Return to %
Play to ⊕ and
skip to Coda)

two. _____ you? _____

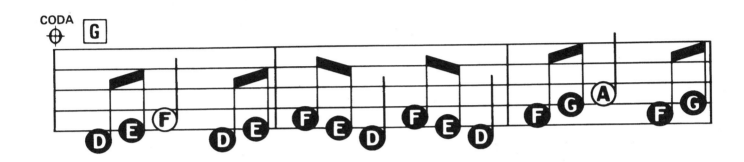

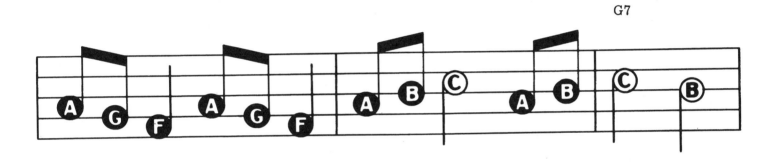

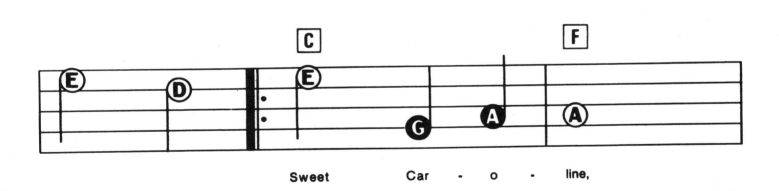

Sweet   Car - o - line,

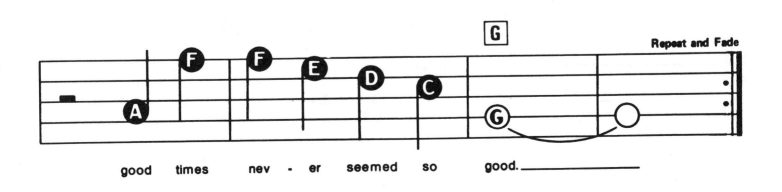

good   times   nev - er   seemed   so   good. _____

This Land Is Your Land

Registration 4
Rhythm: Folk or Fox Trot

Words and Music by
Woody Guthrie

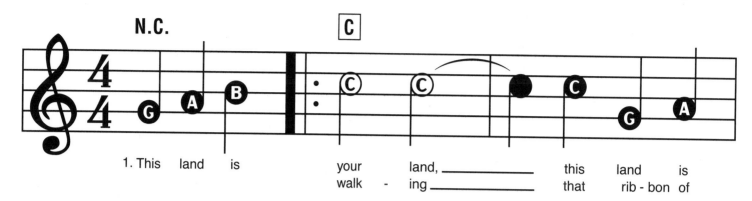

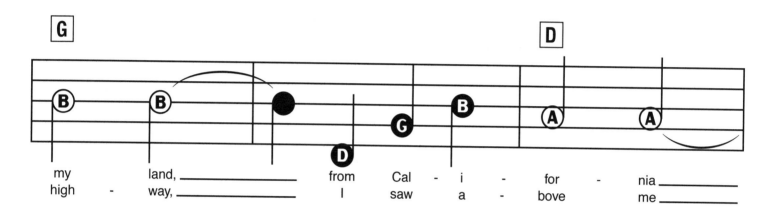

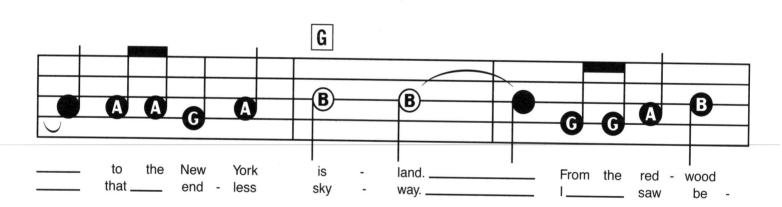

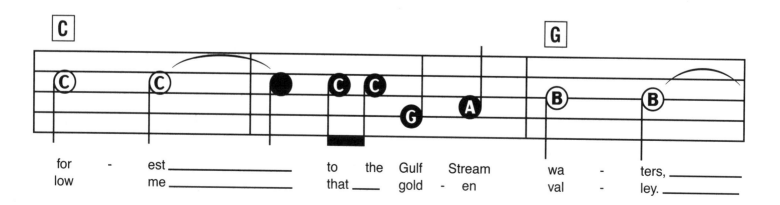

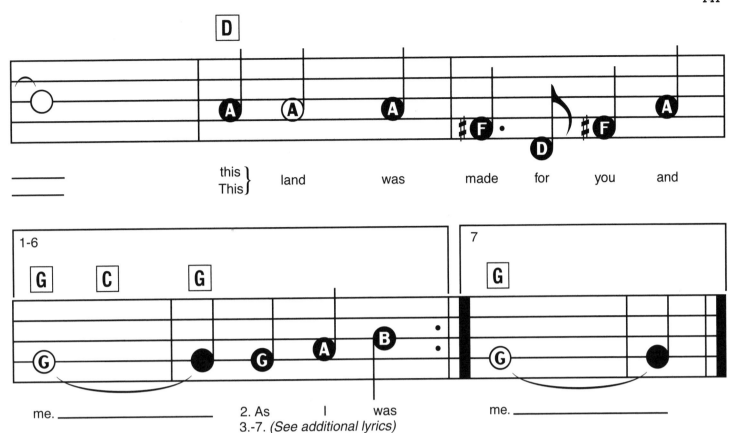

this }
This } land was made for you and

me. _____ 2. As I was me. _____
3.-7. *(See additional lyrics)*

Additional Lyrics

3. I've roamed and rambled and I followed my footsteps
   To the sparkling sands of her diamond deserts;
   And all around me a voice was sounding:
   This land was made for you and me.

4. When the sun came shining, and I was strolling,
   And the wheat fields waving and the dust cloud rolling,
   As the fog was lifting, a voice was chanting:
   This land was made for you and me.

5. As I went walking, I saw a sign there,
   And on the sign it said "No Trespassing."
   But on the other side it didn't say nothing;
   That side was made for you and me.

6. In the shadow of the steeple I saw my people,
   By the relief office I seen my people;
   As they stood there hungry, I stood there asking:
   Is this land made for you and me?

7. Nobody living can ever stop me,
   As I go walking that freedom highway;
   Nobody living can ever make me turn back.
   This land was made for you and me.

Three Little Birds

Registration 5
Rhythm: Latin or 8-Beat

Words and Music by
Bob Marley

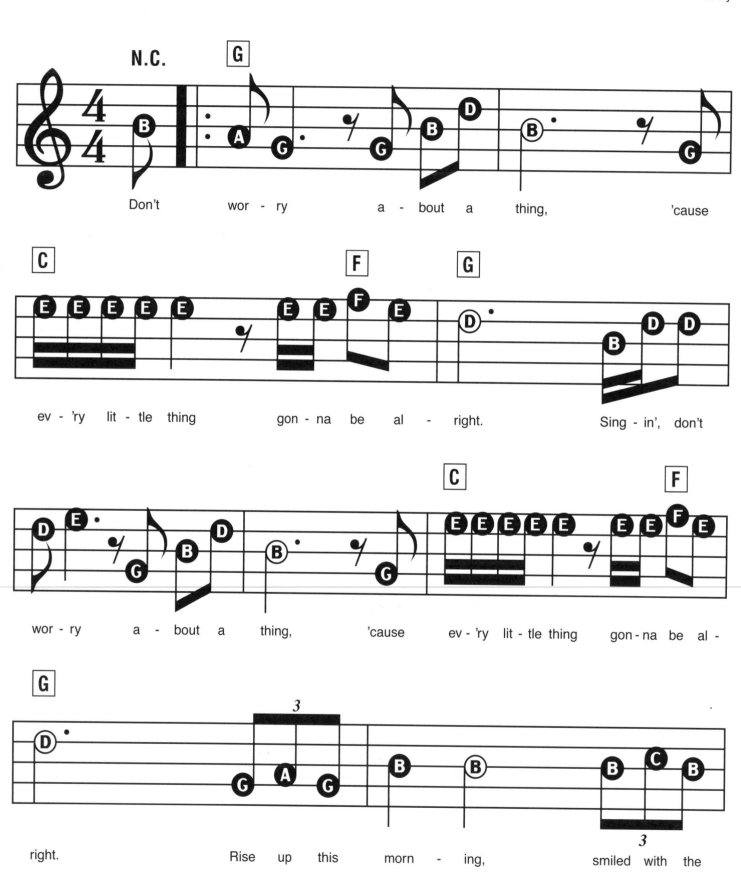

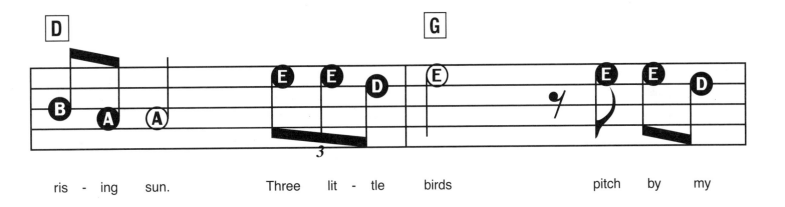

ris - ing sun.   Three lit - tle birds   pitch by my

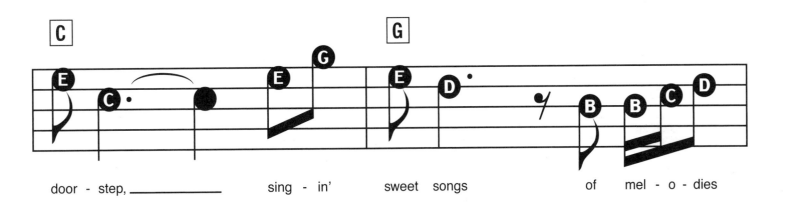

door - step, _____   sing - in'   sweet songs   of mel - o - dies

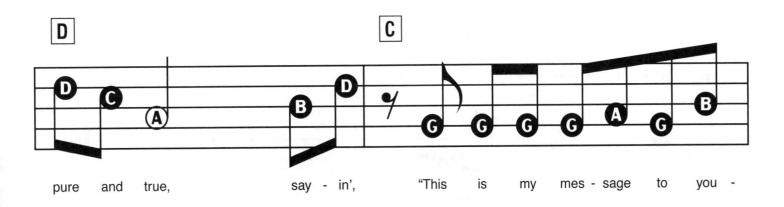

pure   and   true,   say - in',   "This   is   my   mes - sage   to   you -

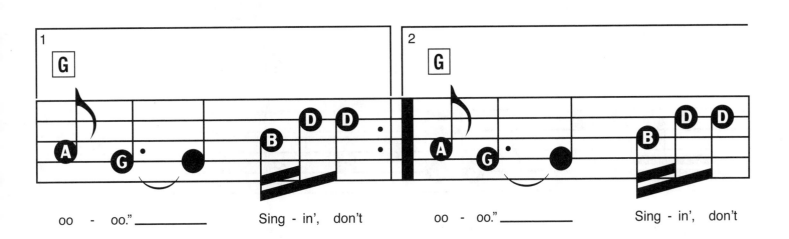

oo - oo." _____   Sing - in', don't   oo - oo." _____   Sing - in', don't

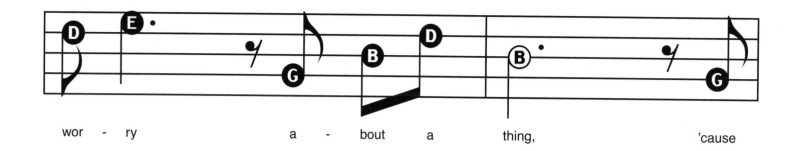

wor - ry   a - bout   a   thing,   'cause

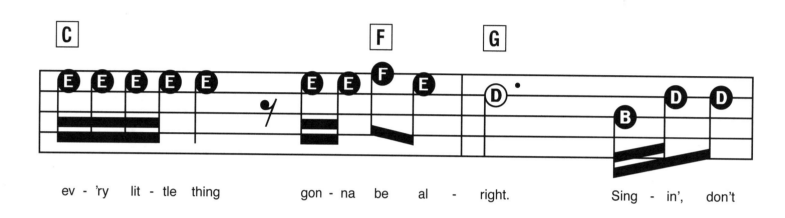

ev - 'ry   lit - tle   thing   gon - na   be   al - right.   Sing - in',   don't

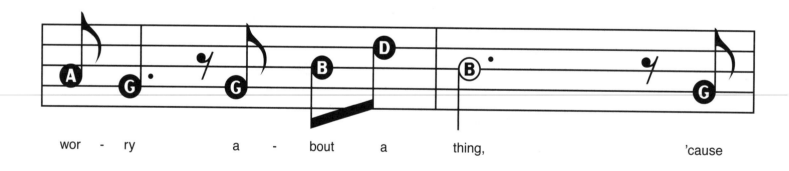

wor - ry   a - bout   a   thing,   'cause

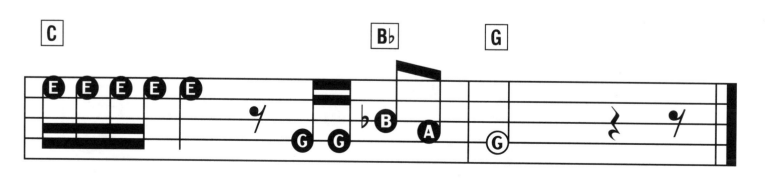

ev - 'ry   lit - tle   thing   gon - na   be   al - right.

Up Around the Bend

Registration 2
Rhythm: 8-Beat or Rock

Words and Music by
John Fogerty

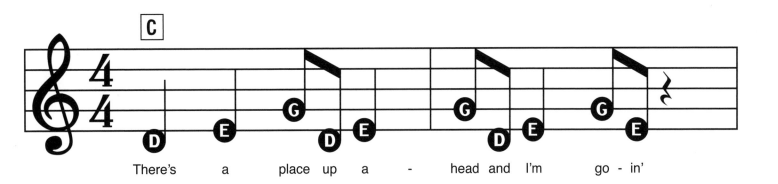

There's a place up a - head and I'm go - in'

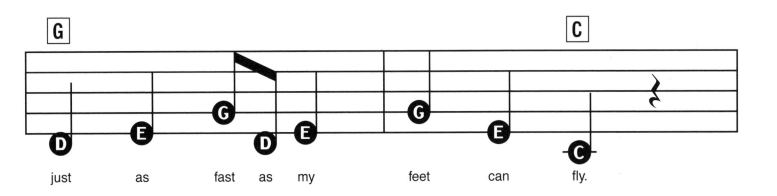

just as fast as my feet can fly.

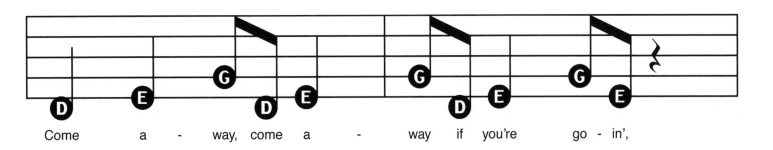

Come a - way, come a - way if you're go - in',

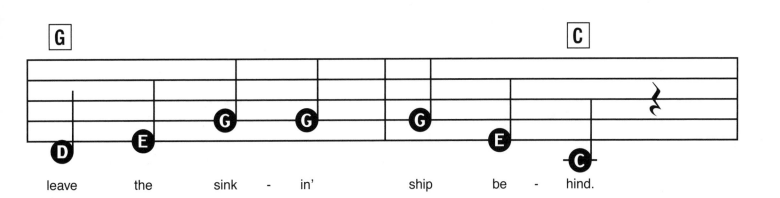

leave the sink - in' ship be - hind.

146

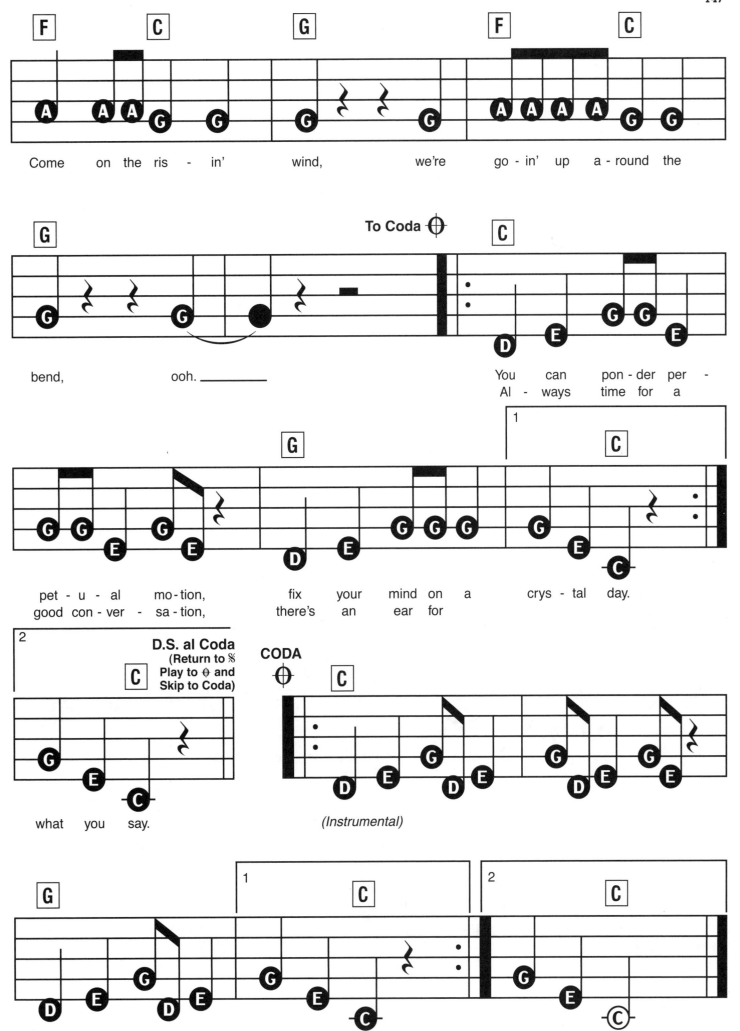

What I Got

Registration 4
Rhythm: Rock

Words and Music by Brad Nowell,
Eric Wilson, Floyd Gaugh
and Lindon Roberts

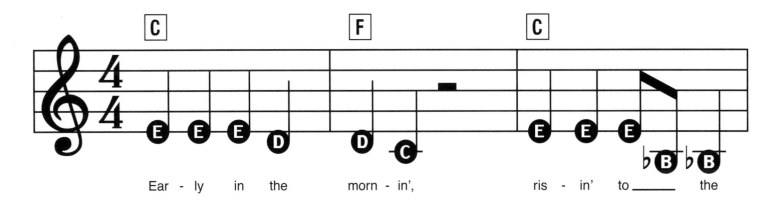

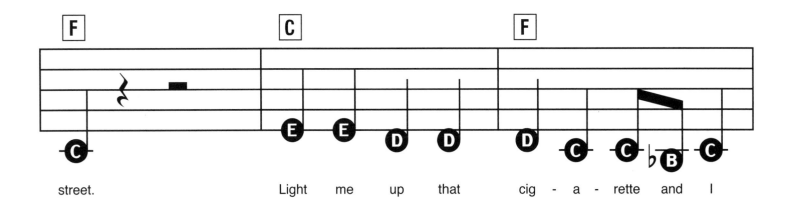

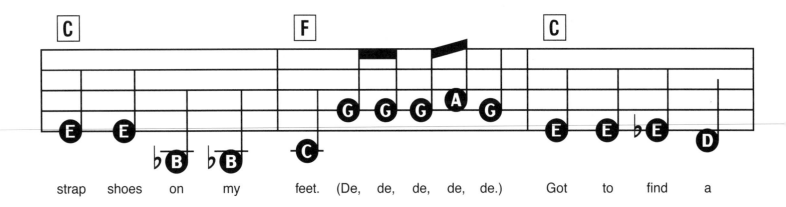

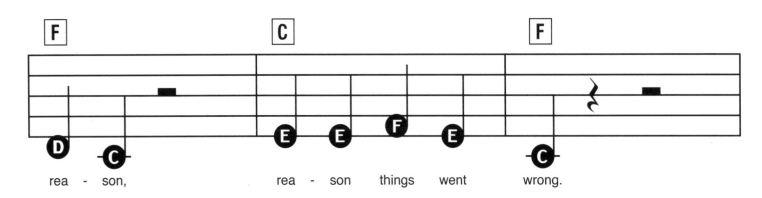

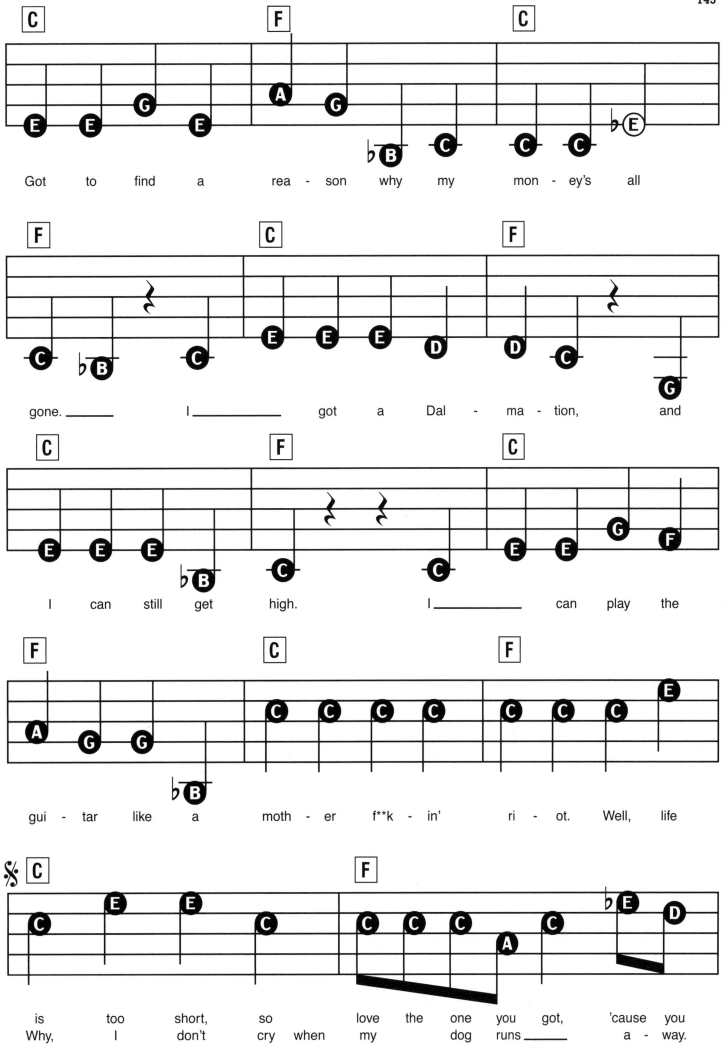

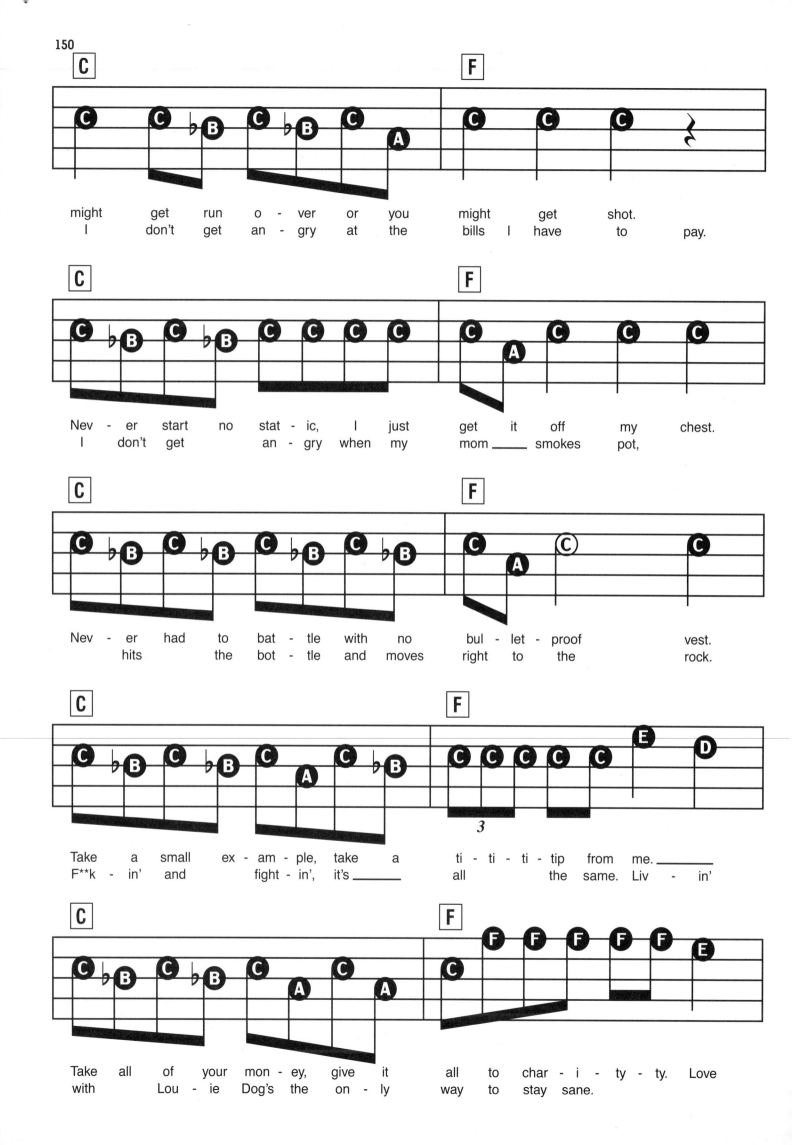

151

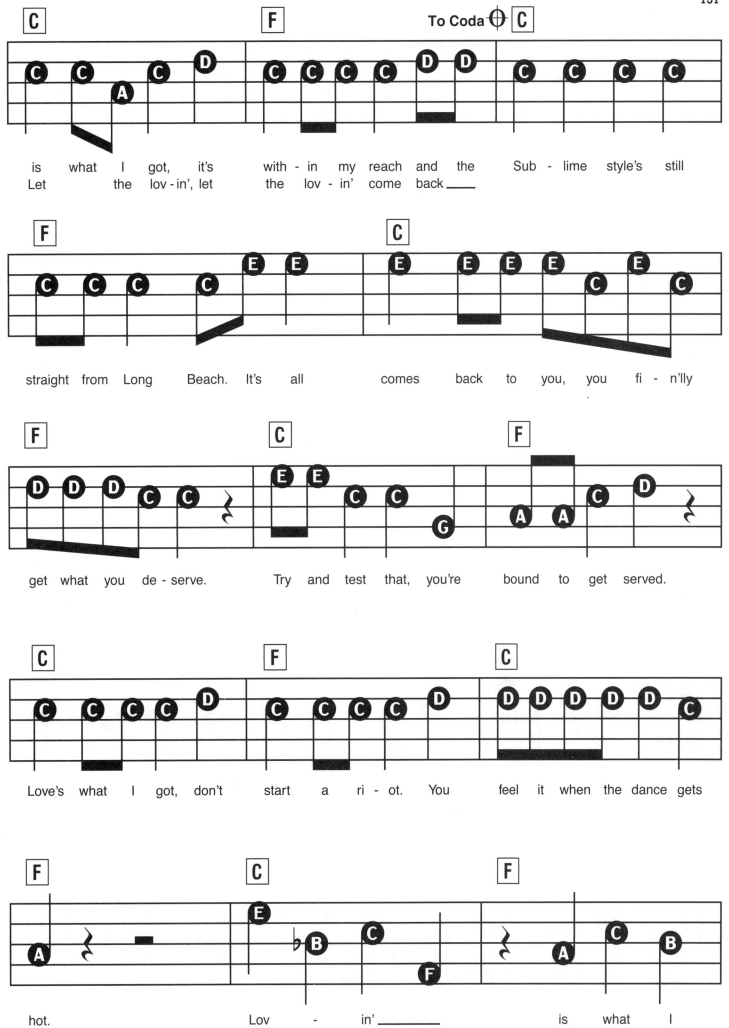

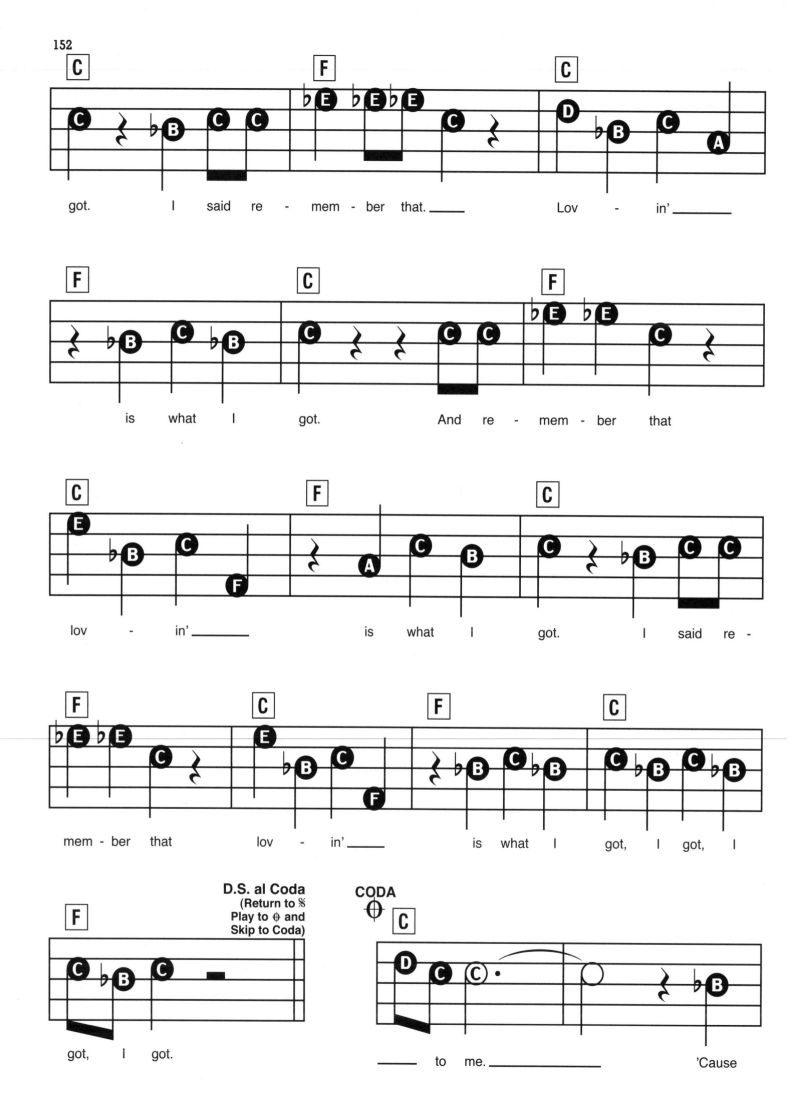

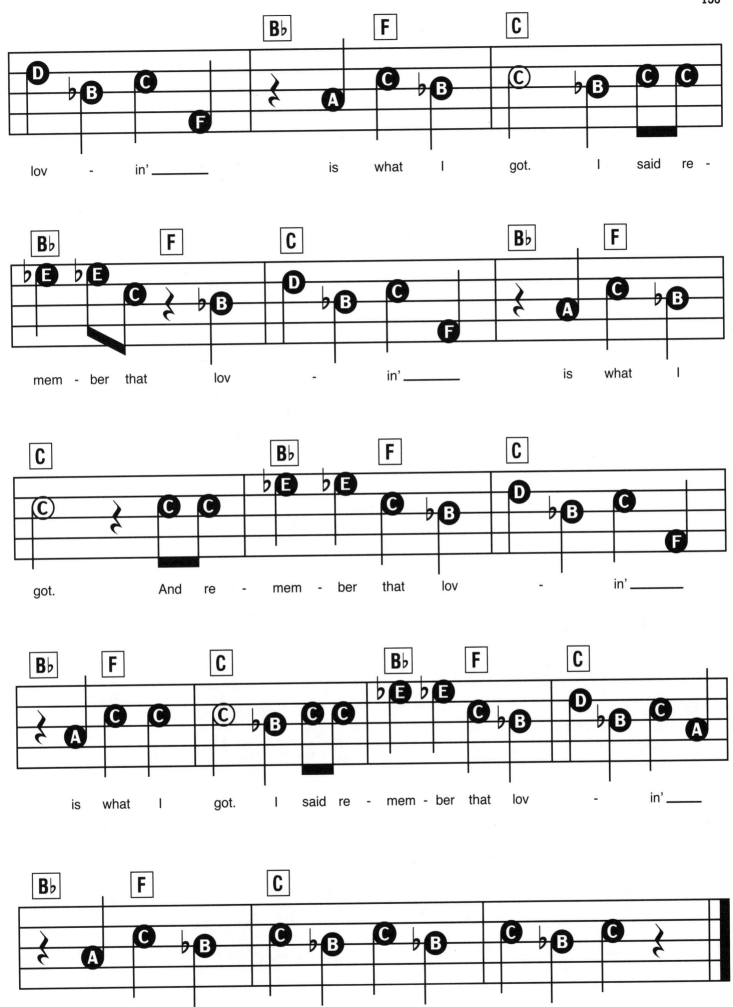

You Don't Mess Around with Jim

Registration 2
Rhythm: Shuffle or Swing

Words and Music by
Jim Croce

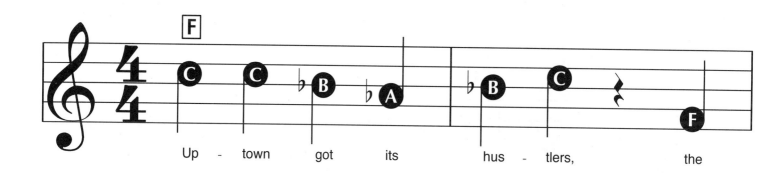

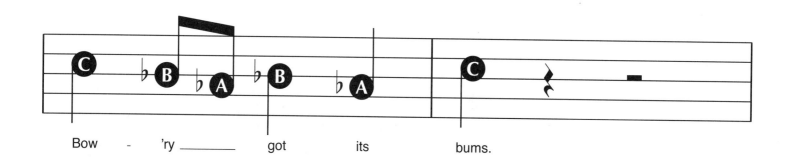

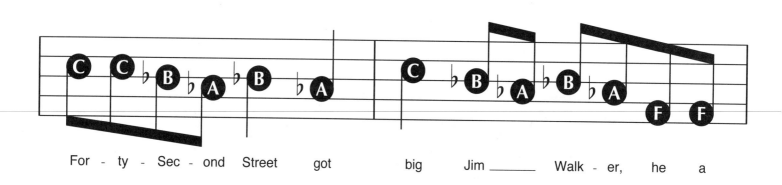

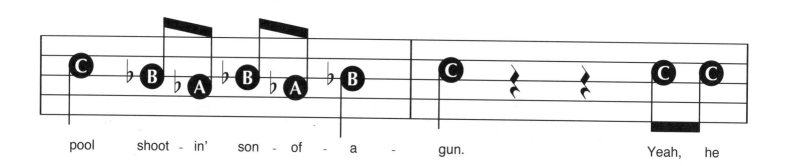

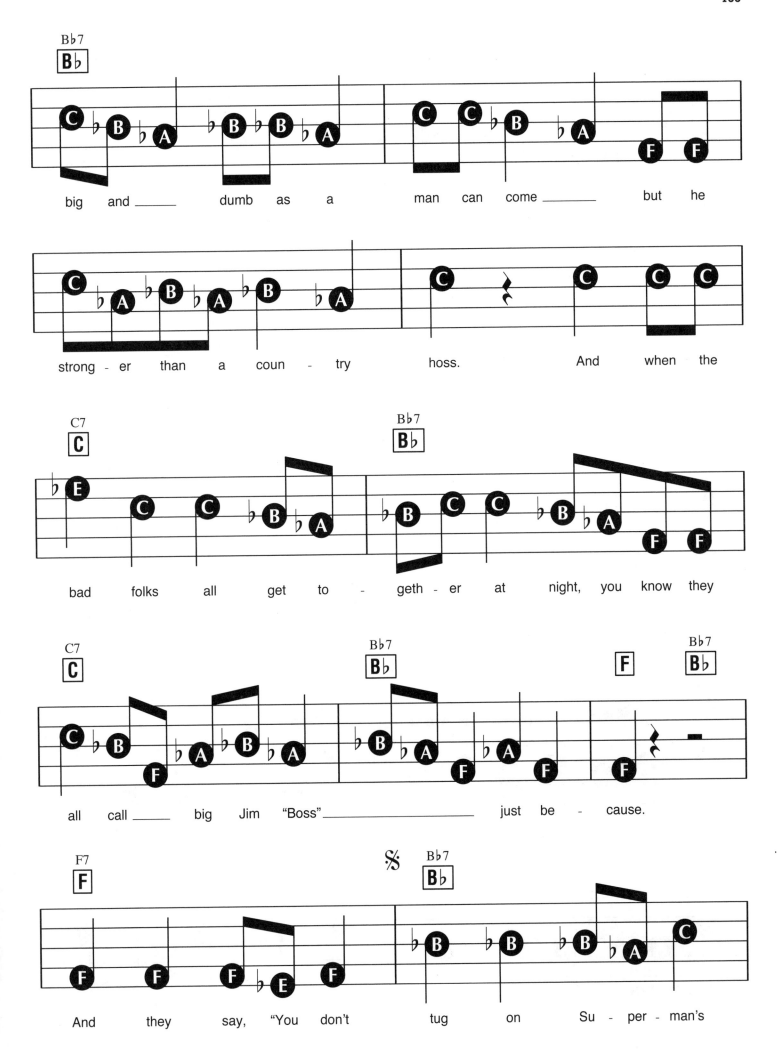

156

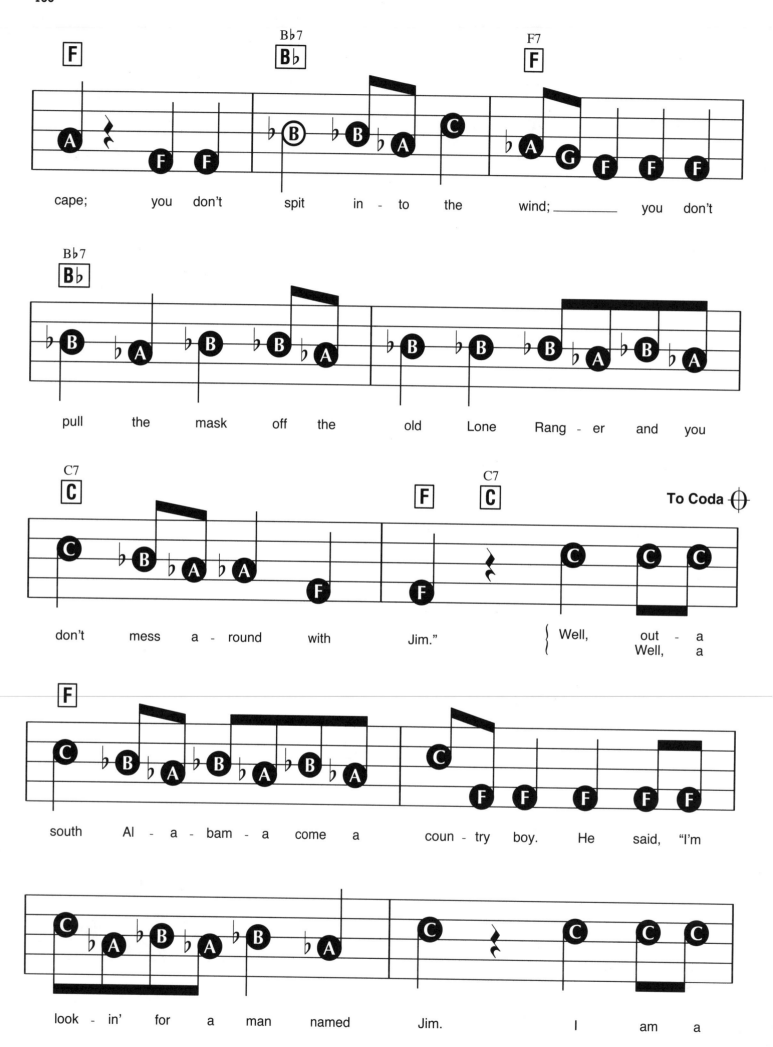

157

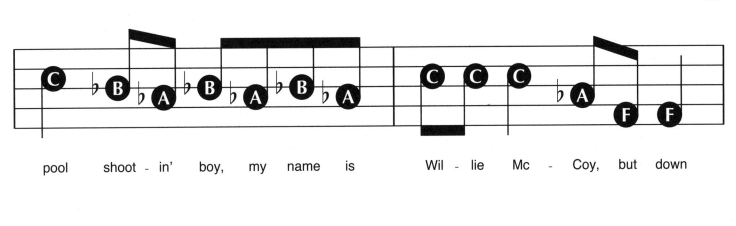

pool shoot - in' boy, my name is Wil - lie Mc - Coy, but down

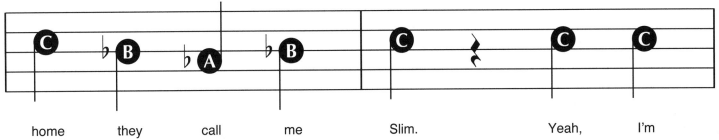

home they call me Slim. Yeah, I'm

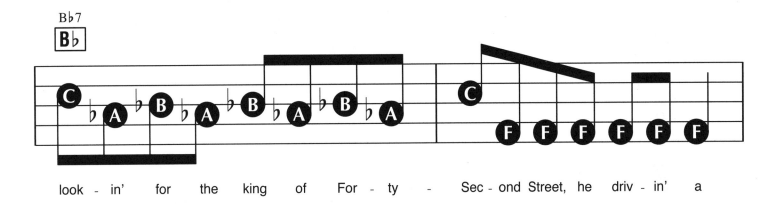

Bb7 / Bb

look - in' for the king of For - ty - Sec - ond Street, he driv - in' a

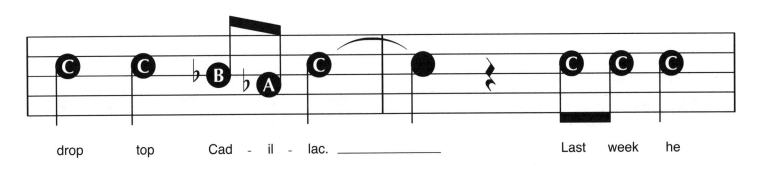

drop top Cad - il - lac. _____ Last week he

C7 / C   Bb7 / Bb

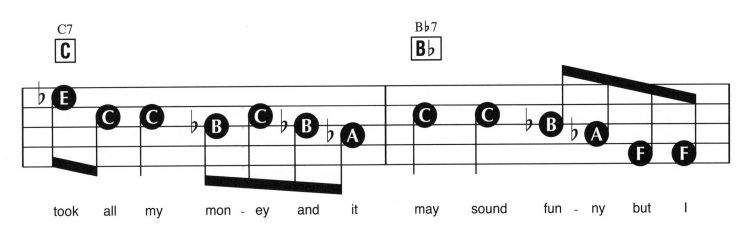

took all my mon - ey and it may sound fun - ny but I

158

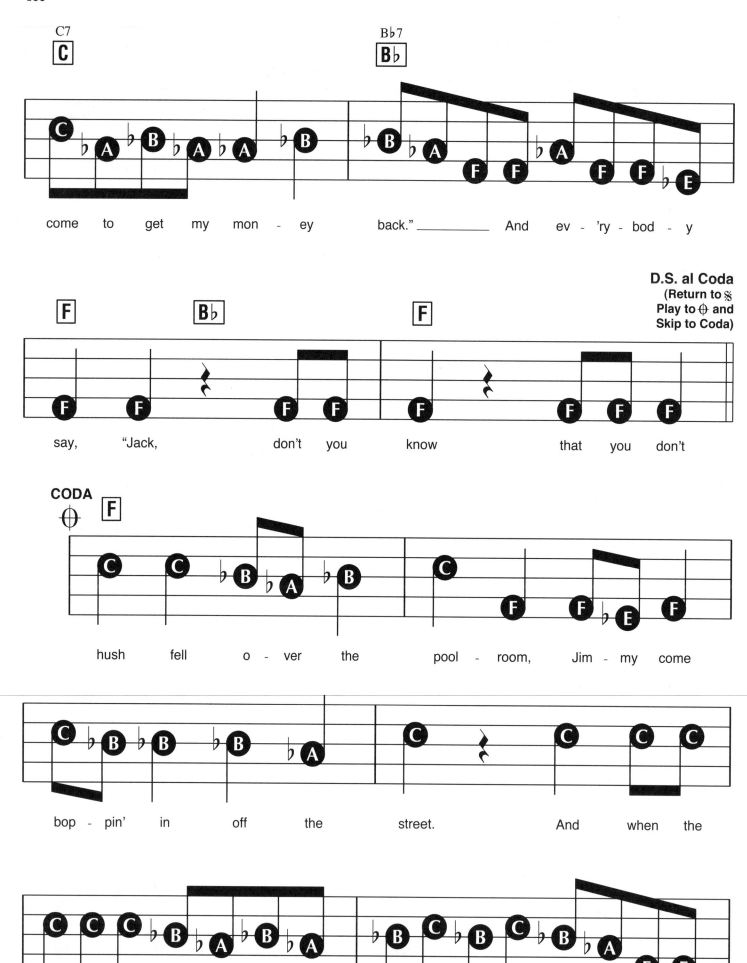

D.S. al Coda
(Return to ℅
Play to ⊕ and
Skip to Coda)

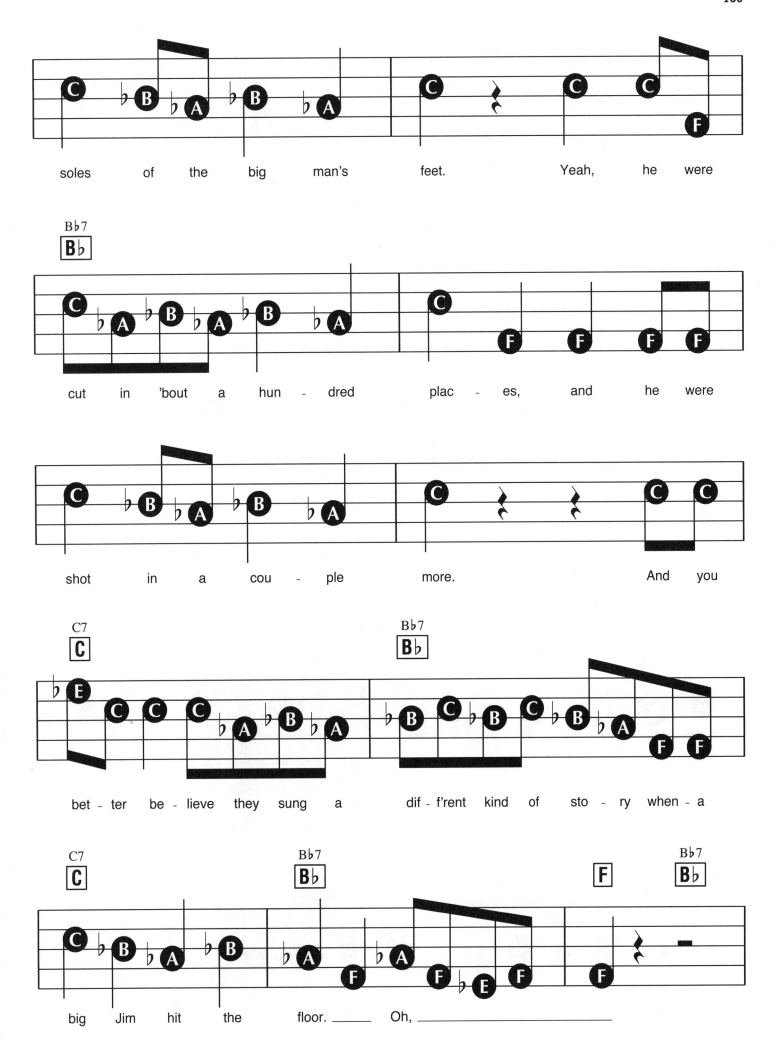

160

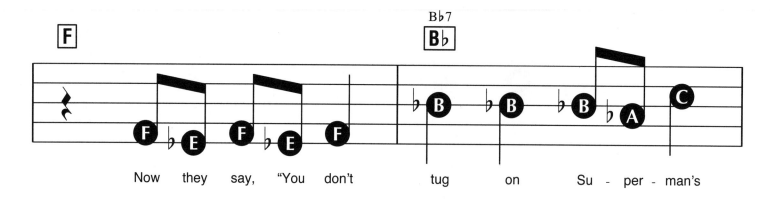

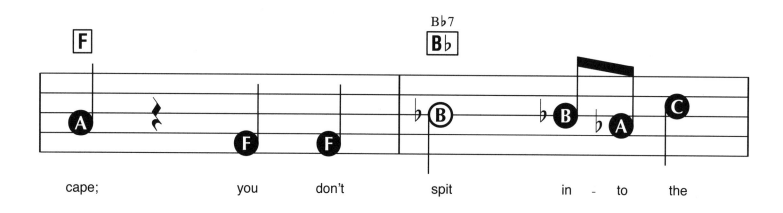

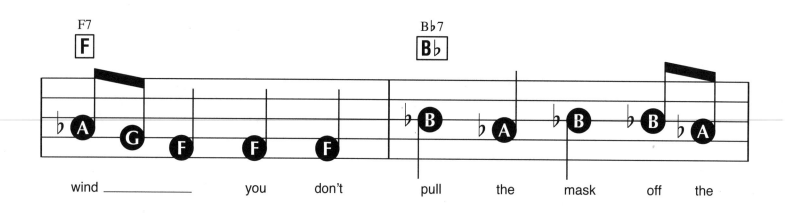

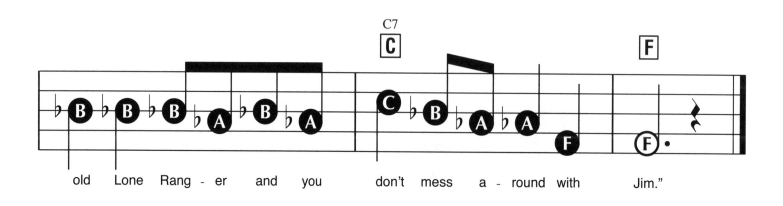